D0049046

PowerLiving by Jake

POWERLIVING
by
JAKE

Eleven Lessons to
Change Your Life

RANDOM HOUSE NEW YORK

Copyright © 1997 by Body by Jake Enterprises LLC

All rights reserved under International and Pan-American Copyright
Conventions. Published in the United States by Random House, Inc., New
York, and simultaneously in Canada by Random House of Canada Limited,
Toronto.

Grateful acknowledgment is made to the following for permission to reprint
previously published material:
Alfred S. Honig & Company: Excerpt from "The Impossible Dream," lyrics by
Joe Darion, music by Mitch Leigh. Copyright © 1965 by Andrew Scott Music
and Helena Music Company. Reprinted by permission.

Library of Congress Cataloging-in-Publication Data
Steinfeld, Jake.
PowerLiving by Jake : eleven lessons to change your life / Jake Steinfeld.
        p.   cm.
Includes index.
ISBN 0-679-45683-X (alk. paper)
1. Success.   I. Title.
BJ1611.2.S683   1997
158.1—dc21   97-21311

Random House website address: http://www.randomhouse.com/
Printed in the United States of America on acid-free paper
24689753
First Edition

To my wife, Tracey, and our children, Morgan and Nicky—my Ultimate Goal every day is to make your lives as fascinating, fulfilling, and incredibly wonderful as you have made mine

To my mom, thanks for always believing

And to my late Go-To Grams, Myra Duberstein, who always took my hand, who always shared my dreams, and who will always be with me

PowerLiving \\'paù(-ə)r-'li-viŋ\\ *n* (1997) : the pursuit of a positive, fulfilling, and balanced existence by exercising control over all the talents, intellectual gifts, and emotional strengths that lie within, thereby creating a dynamic life that is one continuous upward spiral of gratifying achievement

Acknowledgments

I would like to thank Harold Evans and Ann Godoff at Random House, who wisely saw beyond the muscles and got the message.

My thanks go out also to my agent, Jan Miller, who spins success upon success as well as anyone I know.

Although he may not carry a lot of weight in the gym, my collaborator Wes Smith pumps words without peer, and I am grateful for his help in building this book with me.

And, finally, thanks to Wiels, H, Priscilla, Margot, Bette, Morgan, Sean, Dawn, Chuckman, Big L, Teri, McFroy, Big J, Salla, Candy, A-Man, Colleen, Sandy, Keith, Jefferson, Joannsky, and Belly—the gang that started it all for me. I will never, ever forget.

Contents

INTRODUCTION

I've Seen a Lot of Famous People Naked, and They've Got Nothing on You

Our story begins on a gorgeous morning in Beverly Hills, or is that redundant? As usual, I'd completed my own workout before dawn so I could get to my first client's house bright and early. This client was almost always warmed up and eager to get started.

"Let's get it on, Jakey-boy," she'd say before hitting me with the same thousand-watt smile that was lighting up movie and television screens across the country. Like most of my clients, she asked that I come to her house for the workout. They were all either actors, actresses, or studio and network executives who had no desire to be seen by the public the way I saw them.

I've never told anybody about the things I've seen. Until now.

On this morning, as usual, I pulled my black Mercedes convertible into a driveway nearly hidden by shrubbery and trees lining the street in an exclusive Beverly Hills neighborhood. Some driveway. It was more like a boulevard through a national forest. When I reached her house, high atop a hill overlooking Los Angeles, she was not there to greet me, so I went to the door and rang the bell. No answer.

She'd told me before that anytime she wasn't there to meet me, I should just walk in. I was hesitant to do that, but it seemed silly to wait outside, so I went in. I didn't see her anywhere, but I did hear her favorite music pumping from her home gym adjoining the pool.

I found her there, lying on her back on the floor, perspiration dampening her hair and running down her forehead. Her beautiful dark eyes widened as she beckoned me to the floor with her. I was a little intimidated.

This beautiful actress had never been so brazen and uninhibited, nor had she ever exposed herself to me so fully. I had never before seen her so naked in her determination to get in shape.

Gotcha!

You didn't truly believe I was going to write about seeing famous people *naked,* did you?

Hi, I'm Jake Steinfeld, creator of FiT TV, editor-in-chief of *Body by Jake* magazine, and CEO of Body by Jake Enterprises, a multimedia product-licensing and marketing company that grew out of my first entrepreneurial business, in which I served as the fitness motivator to many of the most popular and powerful people in the entertainment industry, including Steven Spielberg, George Lucas, Harrison Ford, Bette Midler, Priscilla Presley, and many others.

Although I pioneered the personal fitness training business and I am an entrepreneur and publisher in the health and fitness industry, this is not a book about *physical* fitness. This is a book about getting fit for a successful, happy, and powerful *life.*

It is important for you to note right now that what has happened to you in the past or even the circumstances that exist for you right now *no longer matter.* From this point on, the quality of your life will change for the better minute by minute, page by page, as you follow the lessons in this book.

PowerLiving involves using your imagination to help you identify goals for your new life. I will also help you create steps that will assist you to go after those goals. If, in the past, you have felt stuck, be prepared to break free of your feelings of helplessness and discontent. Be prepared to experience, perhaps for the first time, a sense of relentless energy, determination, and commitment that will propel you past fears and failures that may have been holding you back.

As you learn to practice PowerLiving, you will find your life suddenly flowing in a continuous upward spiral of achievement and happiness. You will also discover a new sense of self-confidence that comes from maintaining a balance between personal and professional happiness and success. I guarantee that when you complete this book and put its lessons into action, you will like yourself more than you ever have before!

In this book, I will give you not just inspiration and motivation, but also step-by-step lessons and—at no additional charge—useful tools for creating the dynamic and fulfilling life that will allow you to turn your dreams into reality. That is what PowerLiving is all about!

In spite of the name of this chapter, there will *not* be any stories in this book about naked Hollywood stars. (Well, there is one hidden somewhere in here, which I'll get to later.) But if you are looking for a tell-all book, you won't be disappointed. In these pages, I am going to *tell* you *all* that you need to know to immediately get your life on a positive track to your dreams and goals.

One more thing: You will find many references to the word "success" in these pages. When I write and urge you to seek success, please understand that a "successful" life is whatever makes *you* feel happy and fulfilled. It doesn't necessarily mean a bottomless bank account, a six-bedroom house, or a matched set of Mercedes in the garage. It might mean a life of helping other people, or simply a life in which you are constantly using your talents and developing your interests in the most rewarding manner possible. Just as no one else can live your life for you, no one else can define success for you. But I will teach you how to write your *own* success story, based on your *own* dreams and goals.

Believe Me, I've Been There

What do I know about going after dreams? And who am I to be offering you advice? I'll tell you what qualifies me. I'm just a regular guy who is still chasing his dreams and catching some that I had never even dreamed possible. I will be telling you stories from my life throughout this book. For now, it's enough to tell you that I was not always the incredibly handsome, physically magnificent, intellectually astute model of manhood that I am today. (Did I mention "awesomely humble" in there anywhere?)

I was once a fat kid from Baldwin, Long Island, with such a terrible stutter that I was scared to death of having to read aloud in school. I was a below-average student who barely made it through high school and then lasted only one year in college. I moved to Los Angeles at the age of nineteen with nothing more than a beat-up weight bench and a potted palm my mother had given me.

After a lot of stumbling around, some setbacks, and a couple of pretty crazy experiences ranging from a guest appearance with the Village People to a costarring role with Cheech and Chong (more on these later), I fell into a job helping a few people I had gotten to know in Los Angeles get in shape. I taught them how to work out in a way that toned them up quickly and gave them a lot of satisfaction. More important, though, I *motivated* them to do things that they had never been able to accomplish on their own. I discovered that this was my real gift for working with people, and it is what I truly enjoy the most—helping other people lead lives that are more powerful and fulfilling than they had ever dreamed possible.

Back when I began my fitness motivation business, and thereby launched an entire industry in personal fitness training, nobody else was doing this kind of work. While helping out my friends, I discovered that there was an incredible need for this type of service, particularly in Hollywood, where there is so much competition. Most of my early clients were struggling models or actors and actresses who wanted to get toned up physically for television commercials or the occasional shot at a TV show or movie role. But before long, I found myself being sought out by many of the top directors, producers, and business executives in Hollywood. They too were looking for motivation to reach goals that they had been unable to accomplish on their own.

What many of them did not understand initially was that before they could become fit *physically,* they had to change their approach *mentally.* I showed them how to change their *thinking* and the way they *lived,* and then how to change their *bodies.* These clients got into great shape physically, but they also experienced powerful changes in their mental approach to their lives. Suddenly, they were in the flow of life like they had never been before. Word quickly got around Hollywood. Having a Body by Jake became all the rage, and before I knew it, *People* magazine was writing about me and my fitness and motivational techniques.

Although I didn't advertise, hand out business cards, or even have a listed telephone number, the media quickly picked up on my reputation as the Trainer to the Stars, and as a result I became a celebrity myself. It was an incredible experience for a former fat kid from Long Island. It could easily have ended there for me with a couple of clips from *People* and a nice, comfortable life. But it didn't end there, and in this book I am going to share with you the lessons I learned that helped me build not only a very successful business but also a rewarding and balanced personal life for myself and my family.

It's Not Where You Are, It's Where You Are Going

It doesn't matter what happened to you in the past, or what challenges you might be facing right now. What matters is that you believe in your own ability to make your life better. That is such an important lesson, but it is one you don't get in school. You may learn about the French Revolution and the hypotenuse of a triangle, but nowhere in school do they teach you that success is a decision you make.

You can decide to be whatever *you* want, and *you* can do it, but only if *you* believe it and go after it relentlessly. If you are thinking, "*I can't*," you're right. You can't. But if you change that thinking to "*I can*," and then commit to taking positive actions to get what you want, you will do it.

It is all a matter of breaking down the old negative patterns of thought and building up new, positive ways of thinking about your life. The key here is to begin with the understanding that it is within your power to change your life for the better—anytime, anywhere you decide to make the breakthrough.

One thing that makes me confident that I can help you find the way to your dreams is that I *have* seen a lot of famous and successful people naked—in a sense. I have seen them stripped of their public personas, their movie-star trappings, their make-believe auras of confidence and cool. I have gotten to know each of my famous clients as few others do, as real people. I have learned about the obstacles they have had to overcome and the ones they still face. I have seen what drives and motivates them. I realized that nothing comes easy, even to those who may make it look easy. Mostly, though, I learned that these people really are not much different from you and me, and yet they have achieved incredible success once they have learned to be committed to going after well-defined goals with determination, focus, and relentless energy. I helped them learn to *believe* in themselves and their power to control their own destinies.

I remember training Bette Midler to get her in shape for a movie. I'd been pushing her hard one morning. She was near exhaustion, and believe me, Bette lets you know when she thinks you are messing with her. But my job wasn't to be another yes-man, it was to push my clients beyond their limits. So when she told me she wasn't going to do one more sit-up, I told her to do ten more.

"Get lost, Jake, you snake," she said (actually, she said it in slightly more colorful words).

"You're filming in two weeks, Bett-ly. Close-ups. Millions of eyes all over your body. It's up to you," I reminded her.

"I'll give you *twenty-five* more, ya S.O.B."

The Drive to Thrive

Working with these celebrated clients at five in the morning, seeing them all sweaty and straining, I realized they were not gods or goddesses, not heroes, and not really any different from you and me. Sure, they have exceptional talents in some areas, but for the most part they've got nothing on you—other than the drive to thrive.

I came to realize that although many of my clients were extraordinarily talented performers, what really sets them apart is their determination, drive, and dedication. These are people who have taken responsibility for their own success. They don't sit around and wait for a break. They go after what they want with passion and dedication. They are determined to write their own life stories. Many of them came to me when they wanted to begin a new chapter.

Taking Control

I was "given" to Steven Spielberg as a birthday present by a friend, who saw that in order to maintain the pace demanded by his sky-rocketing career, he needed to take better care of himself physically. When word got out around Hollywood that I was training him, people in the entertainment business were in awe. They'd say, "He's the most powerful man in Hollywood. What's he like?"

This was back in 1982, and "Wiels," as I call him, had just done *E.T.*, so he was phenomenally hot in the industry. I was glad to be training him, but at that point in my life, I wasn't likely to be impressed if you hadn't been on the cover of *Muscle Week*. I didn't have any aspirations to be a movie star. I was still in the body-builder mentality, trying to make a few bucks and figure out my next move.

My first impression of Wiels is the way I still think of him today: He is a regular guy without any pretense. The first time we got together, he said, "Jake, go easy on me. The last time I did any physical exercise was in eighth-grade gym class." At first I was just the guy hired to help whip Wiels into better shape, but we quickly became buddies. Soon he was taking me with him on location around the world.

Whether on the movie set in London or flying across the country in a studio jet, Wiels was always without pretension, which made him all the more interesting to me. Because he is such a regular person, I was fascinated by his success and his ability to spin one accomplishment into another. It didn't always come easy for him, but it seemed like he never let setbacks or failures knock him out of his upward spiral. On top of that, he always seemed to be having such a darn good time.

You and I may see Steven Spielberg today as one of the most successful directors in the history of movies, a man surrounded by glamour and power, but in reality he was born in Cleveland, grew up in Phoenix, and was turned down not once but twice by the University of Southern California film school.

That's the naked truth about Wiels. He had to struggle and go through failures before he became one of the world's most renowned directors, and he understands what it is like for others to struggle. As we got to know each other, Wiels and I developed a mutually beneficial relationship. I helped motivate and instruct him on building greater physical strength and a healthier approach to life, while he helped me expand my vision for my own career. He has helped me a lot and he knows it because I tell him so all the time.

Wiels is a powerful figure in the entertainment industry, but he remains a regular guy who taught me that you should never put any limits on the possibilities for your life. Believe me, there are no "overnight successes" in Hollywood or anywhere else. I saw firsthand how hard even celebrities have to work and sweat to compete for roles and to pursue their dreams.

Successful people don't have anything on you; at least, nothing that you can't learn to give yourself. I have written this book to help you take control of your own life and go after what you want with everything you have. When you understand that even the most successful and celebrated people went through years of struggle and scraping to have their talents recognized, it makes you realize that there is no reason to place limits on yourself. The only limitations you have are those you place on yourself.

A Life with No Limits

It was a funny position for me to be in, motivating the rich and famous, since I wasn't exactly the Reverend Billy Graham. But I was good at motivating people beyond the limits they had set for their lives because I had learned how to do it for myself as a bodybuilder.

I thought I had come pretty far from Long Island when I created the personal fitness training industry in Hollywood. But when I saw what those people considered stars or celebrities did when I motivated them, it also inspired me to look at the world without putting any limits on myself. I took what I learned from working with high-achieving, highly motivated people in the entertainment industry and I have been spinning one success into another ever since.

A Little History by Jake

I grew up in a middle-class neighborhood and went to public school. I had nothing special going for me. In fact, I had a few things going *against* me.

I was a bit of a tub. Okay, fat. I was fat. Athletic. But fat. I stuttered, too. It was so bad that I was afraid to call and order a pizza. And you can imagine how much I must have liked pizza!

I overcame my chubbiness and my speech impediment late in high school, and it wasn't by drinking a secret formula like some nutty professor. I did it by taking charge of one small part of my life—my physical conditioning. As I built my body, I built my self-confidence and my attitude about life one step at a time, which is what I am going to teach you to do in this book.

Today, along with having a great wife and two wonderful kids, I am CEO of Body by Jake Enterprises, which was established in 1990 to develop merchandise, programming, partnerships, and other multimedia endeavors promoting healthy lifestyles. I am also the founder, partner, and network anchor of FiT TV, a television network devoted to health and fitness. In addition, my new *Body by Jake* magazine is now on newsstands across the country.

I never dreamed of being a business entrepreneur or celebrity. My Ultimate Goal in coming to Los Angeles from Long Island was to become Mr. America. But along the way I dropped that dream. For me, bodybuilding had always been a matter of hard work and intense training. When I moved up in competition in Los Angeles, I was stunned to discover the widespread use of anabolic steroids to build muscle. This was in 1978, before the negative impact of steroid use was widely known. It shattered my dream, because there was no way I was going to risk my health by taking steroids.

It was a major blow to me, but instead of letting it knock me down, I decided to develop an even greater vision for my life. That vision grew out of my experiences with those in Hollywood who hired me to help them get in good physical condition. The only *nakedness* I am going to write about in this book is the naked determination that you must have to go after whatever it is you want out of life. I saw it in my highly successful clients who believed in themselves and in their destinies. I've lived it myself. If you *believe,* you too will *achieve.*

I believe that you can be anything you want to be, do anything you want to do, and accomplish anything you want to accomplish if you believe in yourself and go after your dreams and goals with relentless energy. I am not saying it will always be easy. We all struggle. We all have challenges to overcome. I prefer to think in terms of challenges rather than problems because "challenge" suggests that whatever is holding you back is not a permanent obstacle. It is something that you will overcome.

For me as a kid the challenge was a bad stutter and a flabby body. For other people it may be bad teeth, big ears, or a bad complexion. It can also be racial prejudice, sexism, a physical or mental handicap, or a tragic or traumatic event.

There is no life without challenge, believe me. Even those rich and famous people you see up on the movie screen, on television, or in the newspapers have had to overcome challenges. Most still face them every day. In the pages that follow, I am going to help you learn how to believe in yourself so that you can overcome the challenges you will face and go after what you want in life. I am going to offer you advice, examples, information, and rules on dealing with the fears that will arise and the risks that you may have to take.

Each of the next eleven chapters offers one of my Eleven Power-Living Lessons. The book concludes with "Two Final Words" that you should never, ever forget as you build that powerful and fulfilling life. Here is a quick summary of each of the chapters:

PowerLiving Lesson No. 1
Believe and You Will Achieve!

Learning to believe and trust in your power over your own life is the first step in the journey. To make this first move, you have to stand in front of the mirror and take a serious look at who you are now, what type of person you have been in the past, what type of person you want to become, where you are in your life now, and where you want to go.

This is a challenging step and it demands that you examine the influences on your behavior, maybe for the first time in your life. To move ahead, you may have to get rid of something that's holding you back or weighing you down. Initially this could be a painful process. Most people, though, discover it is a liberating experience. It frees you to let go of those negative influences and move on to a better life.

PowerLiving Lesson No. 2
Flex Your Imagination

As a kid, I never mowed the lawn alone. There were always thousands of people cheering me on. I visualized myself in Shea Stadium, home of the New York Mets, performing to the roar of the crowd. All of my life I have used visualization to motivate and inspire myself. Before I ever flexed a muscle, I flexed my imagination. Once you have taken a hard look in the psychic mirror and shed the negative influences on your life, then you are ready to flex your own imagination. It is time to shift the focus from looking at who you are to imagining who you can become. Too many people live out of their past experiences and present circumstances rather than looking forward. In this chapter I will teach you how to live out of your imagination by daring to dream for a better life.

PowerLiving Lesson No. 3
Go for the Goal

My guess is that you are interested in making a move on life because now you are feeling *stuck*. Yes. *Stuck.* You may feel like your get-up-and-go got up and went. Or you just may feel like you are drifting in life. That's because you don't have meaningful and realistic goals. One of the things that struck me most about the people

I worked with in Hollywood was that they were goal-oriented. Each and every one of them had mapped out goals, and they never stopped setting those goals higher and higher. In this chapter, I will help you set goals that will have a measurable and positive impact on your life.

PowerLiving Lesson No. 4
Get in the Flow!

Once we get you fitted up with a shiny new set of high-powered, positraction, steel-belted radial goals, you are going to need a plan to put the rubber to the road. Simply having goals won't do it. You need a step-by-step, milepost-by-milepost plan, and in this chapter we will lay that out. Your plan for going after your dreams is important also because, let's face it, this is a long trip and you want to enjoy the ride. In this chapter, I will tell you about scientific research that has shown that the happiest and most creative people are those who have found ways to create *flow* in their lives—a state of mind and way of life in which you continuously move forward and upward from goal to goal and, in the process, create a powerful life for yourself.

PowerLiving Lesson No. 5
Find Yourself a Myra Duberstein

Look, you can't do this alone. Very few people make it without someone cheering them on, someone who believes in you even more than you may sometimes believe in yourself. My grandmother Myra Duberstein was my champion. I've had some others along the way, but she was the main one. She opened my eyes to the world—especially when she took me, when I was ten, to see the musical *Hair*. Not only does having a personal cheerleader make it easier to chase your dreams, it also makes it more fun. Call yours a role model, a mentor, a buddy, whatever you want. We all need somebody to lean on, especially when the going gets tough. Oh, one other thing here. You also have to clear out of your life all those people who may be holding you back. In this chapter I will teach you how to identify both those who can help you and those who may be bogging you down.

PowerLiving Lesson No. 6
Build Your Brand

This is one of my major mottoes. I live it every day and I am going to teach you how to do it, too. It is up to you and only you to build and protect the value of your brand in the world marketplace. What do I mean by your brand? Your reputation and the value you bring to the lives of those you come into contact with. This includes your credibility, character, trustworthiness, and your willingness to offer assistance when needed. The value of your brand is affected by how well you fulfill your obligations in all areas of your life. You have to protect your brand and its value with the same dedication and vigilance that Coca-Cola and other major brand names use to protect theirs.

PowerLiving Lesson No. 7
Success Is a Decision

One of the toughest things about chasing a dream is that you can never find a straight-ahead path. There will always be twists, turns, and challenges. But it is these very challenges that can make you strong, *if* you make the right decisions. When you encounter roadblocks, detours, and hazards along the road, you have to handle these challenges wisely. To do that, you must have a *thoughtful* process for making decisions. How do you decide how to decide? Decide to read this and I'll show you how.

Along with making thoughtful decisions, you've got to master the art of taking *calculated* risks. In this chapter, I'll help you understand the difference between this type of risk, which can be a very good thing, and far more treacherous and foolhardy types of risks. I will also give you a hand in building safety nets so that even when you take calculated risks and fail, you will land without serious injury so that you will be ready to jump up and try again.

PowerLiving Lesson No. 8
Face Your Fears

One of the greatest fears in my life back when I stuttered was being asked to stand up and talk in front of a crowd of people. A few years back, I was forced to revisit and face that fear when I spoke to a national convention of stutterers. Now that is facing your fears in a big way! Before you can actually get rolling on your trip to your Ultimate Goal, you have to sort through your baggage and toss out those fears that are going to hold you back and weigh you down. I know. I had to unload a major piece of luggage. This was like a cast-iron hanging bag. I'll tell you about it in this chapter, and I'll help you find a way to deal with your own fears, whether a fear of failing or a fear of success. Either can be lethal.

PowerLiving Lesson No. 9
Be Like Womba

Who is Womba? Womba was my first big role as an actor, and he died on the cutting-room floor. It was a major kick in the costume for me early in my acting career, but some very good friends helped me see that in Hollywood—and in life—the only thing that can really keep you down is yourself. In this chapter, I am going to share with you the lessons I learned about dealing with challenging times and how to view failure as nothing more than one step in the process of success.

PowerLiving Lesson No. 10
Make a Change and Make It Work

Probably the toughest time I ever went through was when I moved to Los Angeles from Long Island on my own at the age of nineteen. I was chasing my dream, but there were times when I was so lonely and unsure of myself that I nearly packed my bags and went running home. Change is tough, and the inability to handle the emotions and challenges of making a change is another major reason that some people get *stuck* and don't go after what they want in life. This can cause some of the saddest situations I've ever seen. Some people stay in bad relationships or unrewarding jobs because they are afraid to change. They are unwilling to give up what is familiar, even if they are not happy, because they are afraid of the unknown. In this chapter, I will help you learn how to deal with all the challenges that accompany a change in your life.

PowerLiving Lesson No. 11
Commit and Get It!

My father once tried to set me up in his business selling advertising for a local magazine. He even cut a deal with my first customer before I met with him, just to get me off on the right foot. I still walked out without making a sale. Do you know why? I was not *committed* to joining my dad's business. That wasn't where I wanted to go in life. In every mode of transportation, every method for getting from point A to point B, there is at least one critical element. In powerboats, planes, and automobiles, it is fuel. In bicycles, rowboats, and canoes, it's muscle power. In life, it's commitment. To get where you want to go, you have got to be fully, completely, positively, undeniably *committed*. In this chapter, I am going to top off your tank with superpremium unleaded commitment.

Two Final Words
Don't Quit!

Back when I had transformed myself from a flabby kid into a competitive bodybuilder, I thought I was a success. Then I began getting a lot of media attention and making pretty good money training some of the biggest names in the entertainment industry. Again, I thought, I was a success. But guess what? Next, I began discovering and capitalizing on an ever-growing number of opportunities in merchandising and show business. I became very successful at it. I have come to realize that success is not something you achieve, it is something you pursue. In this chapter, I will help you see that a truly *successful* person is someone who is always spinning one accomplishment into an even greater achievement.

In this final chapter, I'll take you over all of the points in the book, and then help you find that one motto, one slogan, one photograph, or one object that you can always keep close by to keep you on track and focused and moving forward. For me, it was a poem that a friend gave me in grade school. It's not Wordsworth or Tennyson, or even haiku, but it changed my life and it still keeps me on track. It's called "Don't Quit!"

It's Time to Get Down to Business

Okay, that's what is in store for you. I will give you the tools to help you make a transformation in your life. They are really good tools. Useful tools. Tools that have worked for me and for most of the people I admire. They are not magical tools. The magic comes when you pick them up and use them in the ways that I will show you.

Are you ready? Let's power up for PowerLiving!

PowerLiving by Jake

POWERLIVING
LESSON NO. 1

Believe and You Will Achieve!

We have established that I was a fat schlump of a kid, with a terrible stutter to boot, but I was not a miserable Sad Sack sitting around the house all day. I had a lot of friends in spite of my pudgy body and my speech impediment. The one thing that was difficult for me to do, other than to stand up and read out loud in school, was to take a long look in the mirror. I felt like an athlete and I was good at sports, but I didn't much look the part. I looked more like Twinkie Boy than Broadway Joe Namath.

My weight problem was not something I really was much concerned about until high school, when girls entered the picture. It didn't even really strike me that I was overweight when I went shopping for a suit to wear for my bar mitzvah. I was thirteen years old, and my mom took me to Syms clothing store on Long Island to get a nice suit for the occasion. I walked in and the salesman gave me the once-over and offered his expert appraisal: "Husky," he said.

He wasn't describing the breed of his sled dog. At that point, I was about five-foot-five squared, meaning I was five feet, five inches tall and about five feet, five inches wide. I weighed around 180 pounds, about 50 pounds of it Twinkies.

After sizing me up, the salesman led me and my mom through the racks of regular kids' clothing to an area where the suits began to look like shower curtains with pockets, buttons, and matching vests. He pulled out a blue suit for me. It looked like something you might hide a movie screen behind. On one sleeve there was a label with the word "Husky" embroidered on it.

"What does that mean?" I asked my mom.

"It means you are a young man now," she said kindly.

I thought that was the greatest thing in the world. Right there on my sleeve. Certification of my young manhood. I wanted to wear it like an admiral wears his stripes. The morning of my bar mitzvah, my mom had to promise me a month's worth of allowance in advance to get me to agree to her removing the "Husky" label from the sleeve of the jacket.

All right, so I was a little out of touch with reality. Who isn't, at thirteen? In fact, how many people do you know in their twenties, thirties, and even their forties, who still haven't gotten with the program?

How many people do you know who are *stuck* in jobs or relationships or places where they feel powerless and unhappy? How many say they don't know what they want to do with their lives, or they don't know where they want to go? How many blame other people for their circumstances? How many are living out of their past and present circumstances because of old hurts or experiences, instead of reaching out for future possibilities?

I have to admit, even after I built myself up physically and overcame my speech impediment, there were still times when my self-image remained that of a chubby kid with a speech impediment. The old insecurities would creep back into my subconscious, and I would have to push myself to shake them off and get back to moving ahead with my life and away from the old Jake, who no longer existed.

Have you ever stopped to think that the only thing holding you back is you? A lot of people are afraid to look in the mirror and really make an honest appraisal not just of their physical appearance but of their character and of who they really are and where they are in their lives. It can be scary, particularly if you go about it honestly. But the only way to clear out the closet is to wade into the mess and start throwing out the clutter and junk that is jamming it up.

Taking Measure

The first step in getting your act together requires that you take some time to assess where you have been, where you are now, and who you have become along the way. If you aren't happy with what you have been getting out of life, chances are you aren't happy with who you are. To change what you are getting, you probably need to change the way you have been going after it.

Because I was overweight and stuttered, I did not have a really good self-image as a kid, but there were a couple of things that saved me from overdosing on Twinkies and going down the tubes. First of all, in spite of my considerable heft and my stutter, I had a sense of humor, some athletic ability, and leadership qualities. What I lacked was the drive to improve my physical appearance and my classroom performance. Like a lot of kids, and a lot of people in general, I was content to go along and get along. I had no goals other than making it to the playground in time to get in the first game.

You can get away with that when you are a kid, but sooner or later you have to kick-start your life by taking control of it. Before you can do that, though, you have to establish what psychologists call self-awareness. To take control of your destiny you have to be honest about assessing your talents and potential and also about the areas where you need to grow and develop greater strength. You have to get a handle on who you are.

Among my first group of clients in Los Angeles was a divorced mother of one child who had moved to town and opened a clothing boutique in Beverly Hills. She was an extremely beautiful woman who had met her wealthy husband while she was still a teenager. She had lived in his shadow for most of her life, but after the divorce she began to come out of her shell, and I was surprised to find that she was very self-assured, savvy, and incredibly funny, too. We had a lot of laughs together, and many long conversations.

I told her she should be a stand-up comic, and she did take on a few comedy roles in movies and her performances were well received by critics. I was amazed at the transformation, and at her determination.

Her ex-husband had died a few years before I began working her out. His estate, which left most of his money to their daughter, had proved to be far less than she had anticipated. But this woman took over management of the estate and in a few short years increased its value from $4 million to $100 million.

Recently, I saw a magazine interview in which my friend Priscilla Presley talked about what made her successful after she divorced Elvis: "It has nothing to do with style or money or trying to emulate someone," she said. "I know who I am, and the values and standards I have. And to know *that* is a kind of freedom."

As Priscilla discovered, creating a successful life is an inside job. Only when you know yourself can you begin to understand the world around you and act effectively within it. In order to get where you want to go, you have to understand yourself first. This involves knowing what motivates you, what holds you back, how you relate to other people, and, most important, why you are the way you are. To one degree or another, we are all a product of many factors. Our position in the family is said to have an effect on our character. You are a product of your environment, your genetic makeup passed on from your parents, and your experiences.

Some people identify themselves by their talents and interests. *I'm a musician. I'm a writer. I'm a dancer. I'm an athlete. I'm a carpenter. I'm a designer.* The talent becomes the basis of their self-esteem, and, in a sense, it is their home base. It can be harder if you haven't identified your talent or area of interest, or if you begin to doubt your talent for some reason. That is why your identity should be based not just on your talent, but on your values and beliefs, your relationships, and your own self-esteem.

I always felt I knew who I was, though I have to admit there was a brief period in my life when I was two people: Jake Steinfeld and Mike Stein.

Back when I was just trying to get my Body by Jake business going, I didn't have an agent to approach clients about endorsements and product licensing. I had built up a pretty good name because of all the magazine articles about my celebrity clients, and I was looking for ways to build the business. I had read about a company out in Lubbock, Texas, that was making a sports drink like Gatorade, and I thought it might be an opportunity to make an endorsement deal. I was still a little shy about calling up and pitching myself, so when I called the company, I lowered my voice a notch or two, down to a Barry White baritone, turned up the New York accent, and introduced myself as Mike Stein, agent for Jake Steinfeld and Body by Jake, Inc.

To my surprise, and Mike's, too, the secretary put me right through to the president of the company, a good ol' Texan, who immediately jumped on the endorsement idea with both boots.

"Mike, y'all come out to Texas this week and we'll sit and structure us a deal," he said.

I agreed, hung up, and panicked. I am a master at disguising my voice, but not my face, so I had to come up with a Mike Stein stand-in in a hurry. I called my attorney, Bob Lieberman, and told him he had to get out to Texas right now and cut this endorsement deal for me.

"I'd be glad to, Jake," he said.

"Oh, Bob, one other thing."

"Yes, Jake."

"You've got to do it as Mike Stein."

Bob said, "No, I'll go as Bob."

This is the sort of trouble you can get into when you try to be someone else. I wasn't trying to con anyone; I just got caught up in a little fib.

Bob went to Lubbock as Bob and when he met with Big John, he said Mike could not make it, but he sent his regards. Big John was willing to talk about the endorsement deal with Bob, but he refused to sign on the dotted line until he'd met face-to-face with his telephone buddy, Mike Stein.

"Ol' Mike and I just hit it off," Big John said. "Tell you what, I'll fly to L.A. next week and meet with you and Jake and Mike, and we'll all have dinner together and make a deal."

Bob flew back and delivered the news that Big John wanted to fly in and meet with the Three Banditos—Bob, Jake, and Mike, our new silent, and invisible, partner.

"Tell him Mike Stein died," my lawyer advised.

Big John rode into town wearing a checked shirt and a bolo tie. Bob and I met him at The Palm restaurant on Santa Monica Boulevard for lunch. Big John seemed glad to meet me, but he kept looking over my shoulder.

"Where's that ol' boy Mike?" he asked.

Bob kicked me under the table.

"He's on location doing some work in Hawaii but he sends his regards," I said. The sweat was running down my forehead. I'm a lousy liar.

Big John studied me. His eyes narrowed. Big John was nobody's fool.

"Jake, you sound an awful lot like ol' Mike," he drawled.

"We grew up together on Long Island," I dodged.

Big John wasn't buying it.

"Jake, let's get down to brass tacks. I want to meet Mike Stein before we do this deal. We really connected on the phone. We are soul brothers. You call me when Mike gets back to town, and he and I will put this deal together. I'll be seeing you."

Needless to say, the deal never got done. I don't blame myself; it was the fault of that darn Mike Stein.

This is an extreme example, of course, of what can happen when you try to be someone you are not.

Sooner or later, someone is going to call your bluff, just like Big John called mine. The solution is to figure out who you really are. Then you can begin to make yourself into who you want to be in order to get where you want to go.

If Toys "R" Us, Who "R" You?

It's been said that the most valuable thing you can know about yourself is to know your own mind. What shapes the way you look at the world? What are the experiences, good and bad, that have influenced the way you have approached your life in the past?

Hold it. Does the thought of taking a good look at these influences make you uneasy? Good! Now we are getting somewhere. If you want to change your life for the better, you first have to understand why you are unhappy, unfulfilled, or discontent with the life you have now. This lesson may not be the easiest to follow, but stick with me—I'm about to take you on your first step toward PowerLiving!

Take a look in the mirror. You don't have to actually stand in front of a real mirror, but imagine yourself holding a mirror up to your life and to your personality. Now ask yourself these questions:

- Do I like what I see?
- Am I where I want to be in life?
- Am I at least headed in the right direction?
- What attitudes, challenges, or people might be holding me back?
- What do I like the most about myself?
- What do I like the least?
- What do other people say about me?
- Of those things I like the least about myself, how do I explain them? For instance, if I am short-tempered, where does the anger really come from? Look within yourself for the true source of it. Do it! Don't be afraid. This is where you need to go, to get to where you want to be.

If you feel that you always have to prove yourself to other people, why are you insecure? Why is it so easy for people to offend you? If you feel that you can never satisfy other people, could it be because you can never satisfy *yourself*?

What I am helping you reach here is a new level of self-awareness. To practice PowerLiving, you must establish a new way of approaching your day-to-day life. You have to take *conscious control* of your thought processes and of the way you respond and react to the world around you. PowerLiving also involves molding your life by changing the mental state that hasn't worked for you in the past and creating new ones.

- What type of person would you like to become? What would you change about yourself if you could?
- What habits, attitudes, and even physical changes could you adopt that would make you a better, happier, and more fulfilled person?

Physical changes? Sure. Your body language defines who you are as much as the words you speak and the thoughts you have. If you sit slumped in your chair or walk like there is a piano on your back, it reinforces an attitude and a demeanor that cripple you. Now, it is entirely possible that you have negative habits, attitudes, and body language that you are not consciously aware of. This is why it can be helpful at this stage to bring a trusted friend into the process. Ask that friend to be honest with you in answering all of the questions you posed. Are your friend's answers similar to yours? What does the friend see in you that you don't see in yourself? I know, it is never easy to see yourself as others see you. It's not easy either to look at yourself honestly. But how you feel inside has a huge impact on how you respond to the world around you. PowerLiving involves improving from the *inside out*.

Changing the Inside to Improve the Outside

I have a friend who is a great stuntman. Early in his career, the word on him was that he was obviously talented but he had a terrible temper and would not listen to instruction. He had difficulty getting work because of his temper and his unwillingness to listen. After a few years he was almost ready to quit the business, until we spent some time together talking about his challenges. First, I pumped him up and told him that he was probably one of the top stuntmen in the business. I told him that there was nothing on the outside to stop him, but what was *inside* was holding him back.

I asked him what made him so quick to anger. At first, like most people, he denied that his challenges with the world came from within. But as I coached him, he went inside and took an honest look. Then, he explained to me that he had come from a troubled family background. I don't need to give you all the details. He confided in me, and I don't believe in breaking confidences. It is enough to know that his anger was rooted in his upbringing and the things that happened to him in the past. People he had trusted had betrayed his trust and disappointed him, and so he had come to expect the same from others, and from the world in general. Understandably, this created a great deal of internal anger and it didn't take much to bring it to the surface.

To help him deal with his anger and his challenges in relating to people, he and I worked on changing what was inside him first. To do that, we started by creating a model for a better way to approach the world—one that didn't anticipate disappointment and betrayal. We worked up what was basically a step-by-step approach for him to follow in going after his next job. I made him throw out all of the internal notions, all of the anger and hostility, and take a new approach. I gave him a new model for introducing himself to his prospective employer. I helped him develop a new way of presenting his background and for dealing with questions.

We restructured his entire demeanor. We had to. His anger had made him all but unfit for dealing with other people. At first he was skeptical. He had tried faking it in the past. But he felt like a phony, he said. He should have. If you don't change what is inside first, you can't fake it on the outside.

He told me my plan would never work, but it did! He got the next stunt job he applied for, and today, I'm proud to say, he is one of the busiest guys in the business. By looking in the mirror, he took the first step to PowerLiving. This talented guy had never before stopped to examine his life and the influences on it. He really had very little awareness that his behavior was generally considered to be out of line. Nor did he understand fully how the negative experiences from his childhood had influenced his perceptions and actions as an adult in such a negative way. But when I helped him become aware of these things, it changed his life forever!

Focusing on Solutions

It is awfully hard to go after what you want in life if you don't understand what motivates you, what angers you, what holds you back, and what pushes you forward. Those inner influences have a great impact on your outer life, and on your ability to create the life you want based on your dreams and goals.

I hated to read out loud in school but it wasn't because I couldn't read very well. I knew the words. It was the inside stuff that was screwing me up. I was insecure about my stutter. That created inner frustration and embarrassment that made the problem worse.

Because of my insecurity, I would rather have jumped off the Empire State Building naked than read out loud in class. I might have ripped right through the story when reading to myself, but when it came time for me to read out loud, I'd panic. I would read ahead and try to practice the words in my mind so I could get them out, but in doing that I'd miss the context of what I was supposed to be reading.

My mind knew the words, but I couldn't say them. My frustration and embarrassment over my stutter held me back in school. It really turned me off to school, except for the social stuff and sports. I know that now, but I didn't really understand the reason I was so uncomfortable in school. If I had been more aware of it, I might have been able to do more about it. That's the value of self-awareness. When you reach an understanding of why you act the way you do, it gives you the power to do something about it. Things that happen to us in life affect us in ways that we sometimes are not even consciously aware of. If someone or something hurt us or scared us as children, we can carry strong feelings about the person or thing into adulthood. Those deep-seated emotions can affect the way we look at things or respond to people years and years later. Unless we have a certain level of self-awareness, we may not understand why we react the way we do. This can affect jobs, relationships, and many other aspects of our lives.

I have a friend whose front teeth were knocked out when he was in Little League because a ground ball took a hop and hit him right in the mouth. For the rest of his life, my friend could not go after a ground ball without turning his head away. He couldn't help it. That memory of getting hit in the mouth by a hard grounder—not to mention all of those trips to the dentist to repair the damage—had imprinted a message in his brain: "Protect your face!"

It didn't do much for his fielding, but he certainly was aware of why he reacted that way. That's a relatively minor challenge compared to other responses that become programmed in our subconscious because of past hurts or experiences. Imagine someone who has had a far more serious injury or emotional trauma and you can start to understand how important it is to strive for self-awareness in order to resolve deep-seated conflicts, or at least to know the source of them.

While identifying the things that hold you back may not make you overcome your challenges immediately, at least it is a start toward moving away from the challenge and toward the solution. That is a key step in taking control of your life. Challenges weigh you down. Solutions move you forward.

To compensate for my stuttering, I worked hard at being one of the guys and being good in sports. The thing that really changed my life, though, was weight training. For me, and for many people I know who do weight training, it was not really about building strength—it was about establishing control over my life for the first time. I was fifteen years old the summer my father bought me a set of weights. He called me out to the backyard and said, "Let's do some bench presses." I looked down at my Twinkies and said, "No thanks, Dad." He had been in the U.S. Navy and he was an all-around tough guy. You didn't mess with my father, though he was a softy at heart. He asked you to do something only once. He didn't push, he only suggested. He always left it up to me to follow through. I realize now that he was trying to teach me to take responsibility for my own life.

The weights and bench sat unused in the yard most of the summer. Then, in the fall, my father told me to move them into the laundry room, just off my bedroom in the basement of our split-level house. I hauled everything down there and left it in a pile. I didn't pay any attention to it again, until one night after school had started. I was a sophomore then, and I was supposed to be reading social studies and highlighting the important stuff, but mostly I was just turning the pages of the textbook. I always had trouble with the concept of highlighting because I could never decide what was supposed to be important. I couldn't make the distinction either in my studies or in my life at that point.

I'm not sure what made me get up and start messing with the weights one night. It was probably boredom with social studies.

But suddenly there I was, wearing a skinny tank top with my flabby belly hanging over my pants, standing in front of the full-length mirror on the door with the weights in my hands.

I'd been listening to music on my headphones and still had them on. I'd put on a recording of Frank Sinatra singing "My Way." The lyrics were inspiring, but what really got me was what came right after the song. There was about a minute of wild applause and cheers from Frankie's fans. In my imagination, I decided they were cheering for me as I pumped iron. I started doing bicep curls with the barbells as they cheered me on. There must have been fifty thousand fans in Madison Square Garden cheering me on.

With my fans cheering me on, I forgot all about the weight of the barbells and focused instead on the rewards I was reaping. As corny as it sounds—and I know, it sounds pretty darn corny—that little impromptu weight-lifting session marked a turning point in my life.

Suddenly, I was no longer hung up on my challenges. Instead, I was focused on working toward solutions. When I got up the next morning, I was still an overweight kid on the outside, but on the inside I was already well on my way to a major change. I had not been able to control my stutter and my insecurity, and that probably had contributed to my overeating. But here was something I could control. Already, I could feel the tightness in my biceps. It may have been nothing more than a little soreness that first morning, but it gave me a sense of growing strength. It was something that *I* had controlled by taking an action. I could feel the direct results.

I have a very clear memory of the next weeks and months of my life. I remember every day going to school and just feeling different about myself. The change started first in my head and in my attitude. I walked with more confidence. Instead of keeping my shirt untucked to hide my belly when I sat down, I tucked the shirt in and kept my chest out and shoulders back. I could feel the tightness of the muscles, and soon, others began noticing too. Suddenly, Jake was no longer just this funny, soft-bellied guy. I'll never forget the first time one of the guys said, "Jake, what's with the biceps, man? You been workin' out or sumptin'?" I especially remember the first time one of the girls came up and said, "Ohhh, Jake, you've got muscles."

When other people started noticing the changes in my body, my life took on a new purpose beyond the next ball game or a Twinkie and a Coke. I had a goal. I began working out every night with Sinatra and our fans in my basement bedroom. It was the thing I looked forward to the most each day. Building strength became my passion. I must have watched every Hercules movie ever made. I bought bodybuilding magazines and I began ordering stuff from Charles Atlas. (By the way, Charlie, I'm still waiting. You owe me a buck fifty plus stamps.)

It had dawned on me, *I can change my life doing this.* When I realized that, I went from zero to hero.

I didn't need much more encouragement than that. I'd never had such a feeling of control over my life. I learned that I didn't have to be Twinkie Boy if I didn't want to be Twinkie Boy. I learned that by making a power move to improve my physical condition, I could achieve not only that but reap other benefits as well. I could envision what I wanted to look like in the mirror, and then I could become that picture in the mirror. I could build value for myself and in myself.

Weight training is not the only way to take control of your life and to build value in it, of course. I am certainly not preaching that you have to run out right now and start pumping iron. The point is that for me, weight training led to the realization that I could control my circumstances. It helped me believe in my own power over my life. Once I believed in that power, it made me want to achieve even more.

Turn Your Butterflies into Eagles

Imagine two guys in a race, Ted and Ned. They are at the starting gate waiting for the "go" signal. Positive Ted is thinking, "This is it. This is what I've been waiting for. I am so psyched and ready. I'm not only going to break the record, I'm going to break the sound barrier!"

Next to him, Negative Ned is thinking too. "Man, this cross-wind is going to slow me down. I'm not at my best in hot weather like this. I should have had more carbohydrates last night. I'm not feeling charged up enough."

Not much doubt about who is going to win this race, is there? Having a negative attitude is like carrying a piano on your back. It slows you down. It causes you to give up even before you've started. Attitudes are like magnets. They attract what you put out. If you carry around a negative attitude you attract negative people and negative things. It's like someone who doesn't take a shower for a couple of weeks. The only people who can stand to be around him will be other people who haven't showered. If you put out negative vibes, that is what will come back to you.

Positive people, on the other hand, seem to have wings on their backs. They can't wait to get up in the morning and get going. When they hit an obstacle or hard times, they go at it with a full head of steam. It may slow them down, but it doesn't knock them down. They believe in their power to achieve positive results. They make things happen in their lives. Even when positive people lose, they take what lessons they can from the loss, learn from them, and move on. Have you ever heard a lifelong winner like Joe Montana or Michael Jordan or someone you know personally talk about losing? Listen closely the next time you're with this person. What you hear will be something like this: "I lost this time, but I learned a lot that will help me do better next time." Or this: "I'm just going to think about what happened today, so that it motivates me and makes me better the next time."

Lifelong winners practice PowerLiving. Even when they lose, they win, because they take something positive out of the experience. They lose, they learn, and they move on, determined to keep that upward spiral spinning. That is PowerLiving.

A positive attitude builds perseverance, which is something you are going to need when you go after your dreams and goals. Say you want to learn to play the guitar. If you have a negative attitude about practicing, you'll never make it through the first few months of frustration as your fingers fumble around the strings. But if you are positively charged, you will tell yourself that everyone, even

Eric Clapton, fumbled with the strings in the first few months, and you will keep on going.

Don't get lost in the challenges of today; think of where you are going so that minor setbacks don't destroy the dream. A lot of people come up against a challenge and say, "That's it, they told me no. It's over."

No, it's not over. Not if you believe that you can achieve your dreams.

POWERLIVING
LESSON NO. 2

Flex Your Imagination

When I was kid, thousands of fans cheered whenever I mowed the grass in the backyard. The cheering and chanting usually began as soon as I wheeled our lawn mower out of the garage and knelt to pour gas into it. That alerted the public-address announcer at Shea Stadium, who would announce, "Ladies and gentlemen, boys and girls, starting today in center field, the man with the mightiest mower in Baldwin, Long Island: JAAAAAKE STEINNN-FELLDDD!!!!"

They really loved it when I yanked on the rope to start the mower's engine.

"MOW, JAKE, MOW! MOW, JAKE, MOW!"

My fans were always there for me. When I cleaned my room, they roared. When I lifted weights, they were in absolute awe. When I . . . Okay, you get the picture. As a kid, I had no lack of imagination. I hated mowing the lawn, so in my mind, I wasn't mowing the lawn, I was prowling the outfield of Shea Stadium in search of fly balls and line shots with thousands of people cheering my every move.

It was just my imagination, of course, but do you know what? When I began to dream that I was capable of doing exceptional things, then it began to seem entirely possible that I *could* do exceptional things. That is the power you unleash when you flex your imagination by using it to elevate your life from the mundane to the magnificent.

Living Forward Without Looking Back

Most people who are dissatisfied with where they are in life feel that they aren't getting anywhere. They feel stuck. They feel that their lives are controlled by their present circumstances or their past experiences. *I can't get ahead because this job doesn't pay enough and I don't have enough education to move up. I'll never find someone who loves me because if it hasn't happened by now, it never will happen.*

Sound familiar? That defeated, stuck-in-the-mud state of mind is typical for someone whose view of life is focused backward instead of forward. They are using their imagination, but they have it pointed in the wrong direction.

Losers imagine how they can fail. Winners dream up ways to succeed. Losers focus on their past failures. Winners look ahead toward success. People who can't get over what has already happened to them are like someone trying to drive a car with both eyes trained on the rearview mirror instead of looking ahead through the windshield.

Many people think their memory is a window to the future, when in reality it is only a storeroom for the past. Your memory tells you only what you have already done. It tells you what your limitations have been, not what your potential might be.

To take control of your life and move it forward, you can't live according to past experiences or even current circumstances. The way you change your focus is to look forward through your imagination to the greater possibilities for your life. Your imagination is an incredible tool, but like most tools it can be used to build or to tear apart.

When used properly, your imagination provides you with dreams that are your doors to future achievement. It tells you what can be done if you have the courage to close the door on the past and open the doors to greater success. With your imagination, you can create the life you want because when you flex your imagination it builds an image in your mind so that what you want becomes far more than a simple *dream,* it becomes a *certainty,* a mission that is entirely possible.

Mission Possible

Do you know that for thousands of years it was commonly accepted that no human being could run a mile in under four minutes? No one had ever done it in the past, so it was assumed no one could do it at all. Because of this limited thinking, it wasn't until 1954 that an Englishman by the name of Roger Bannister finally broke the four-minute mile. Bannister said he did it by spending years and years *imagining* himself breaking through the barrier so that in his mind the limitations were wiped out. Breaking the four-minute mile became not just a dream, but a real possibility for him.

The really striking thing about this breakthrough was that once Bannister did it, with a time of 3:59.4, and proved it was possible, thirty-seven *other* runners broke the four-minute-mile barrier within the next year. What does that tell you? That most of the barricades and limitations that you put up come out of your imagination, and so you can break through them by flexing that same imagination.

Mastering Your Imagination

In the previous chapter, I advised you to determine who you are by examining your past experiences as well as the events and attitudes that may have influenced the way you look at the world and the way you treat other people. The next step is to consider what type of person you want to *become* and what you want to do with your life.

The key to changing your life for the better is to stop living on the basis of your memories of the way things have been in the past, or even of the way things are right now. Instead, you need to begin flexing your imagination by *living forward*—to the way you want things to be. It is a power that we all have, a magic we can summon, if we simply change our way of thinking.

Too often, people continue to do things that they know are self-destructive simply because they can't imagine behaving any other way. How many times have you heard someone say that a friend or loved one will wake up once he or she "hits bottom"? Why does it take a disaster or some great slap in the face to wake up someone who is engaged in self-destruction? Why do they have to get fired or go bankrupt, nearly die, or lose a loved one before the alarms go off?

Why is it that so many people fail to realize that the only way to change the results you have been getting in your life is to change the way you have been living? It seems so obvious: If it hurts when you bang your head against the wall, you should stop banging your head.

Often, people can't see a way out of bad habits or destructive behavior because they have not learned to tap into their imagination. Admittedly, it isn't easy to get rid of bad habits, but the strongest weapon you have against them is your ability to imagine a better life.

Ready, Aim, Imagine

When I was training celebrities and Hollywood executives, one of the best ways I had to motivate people was to trigger their imagination. Some of the people I worked with had not engaged in physical activity for years. Some had been chronic smokers or overeaters. Most were intelligent people who realized their bad habits were dangerous to their health. Often they had tried different methods to stop their harmful behavior. Things like nicotine patches or fad diets worked only for the short term, if they worked at all. The clients who were most motivated to change their bad habits and get fit were those who had had a scare that triggered their imagination.

Your imagination is a powerful tool not only for breaking bad habits but also for creating a greater vision for your life. An old friend from the neighborhood reminded me recently of something I used to do as a kid. I'd forgotten about it, but he hadn't. He said that he wasn't surprised that I've been successful because he remembered me standing in the backyard back in Baldwin, belting out verse after verse of one of my favorite show tunes: "To dream the impossible dream, to fight the unbeatable foe, to bear the unbearable sorrow, to run where the brave dare not go. This is my quest . . ."

He said it drove the neighbors crazy. I'm sure it did. I've got nothing on Robert Goulet, but I have always been the master of my imagination. Growing up, I was a big dreamer. I'd lie in bed and see myself on a float in the Rose Bowl Parade, or playing power forward with the Knicks at Madison Square Garden. All kids do that, I know. But there is a big difference between the kids who simply have such dreams and the kids who believe that their dreams can become a *reality*. I believed then, and I believe now. Why shouldn't I? Believing in dreams has been very, very good to me.

Believe In Your Dreams

As an adult, I have different dreams, of course. Now, instead of dreaming about taking a pass from Walt "Clyde" Frazier and making a slam dunk, I am more inclined to dream about making the Fortune 500.

Adults tend to think that "using your imagination" is kid stuff. I'm here to tell you that they are wrong. You are probably aware of the fact that Steven Spielberg is a partner in a new company called DreamWorks. That's not just some whimsical name created to be cute. Wiels is one of the biggest dreamers I know. He used to dream that I wouldn't show up and torture him when I was his fitness trainer. He once told an interviewer that working out with me on Mondays, Wednesdays, and Fridays made him appreciate Tuesdays, Thursdays, and Saturdays more than he ever had before.

Wiels, whose movies have grossed more money than those of any other director in film history, is also one of the world's greatest examples of someone who has created an incredibly successful life by flexing his imagination and bravely following it, wherever it has taken him. If his movies often seem to have a magical quality, it comes from his imagination. Wiels definitely knows how to live out of his imagination. Today he seems to lead a charmed life, but the truth is he is really not that different from you and me.

Following Your DreamWorks

One night many years ago, an engineer in Phoenix, Arizona, who was an amateur astronomer and science-fiction buff woke up his six-year-old son while the boy's mother and three sisters slept. "I'm taking you to see an extraordinary show" was all the father said.

Scared, but excited too, the boy was silent as he and his father drove for a half hour into the dark desert. Finally, they reached the rim of a canyon more than a hundred other parents and their children had driven to. People were sitting and lying on blankets, gazing up at the sky at what the boy would remember as a "phantasmagoric" meteor shower. It was a cosmic fireworks show and it ignited the imagination of little Wiels. The creator of *Close Encounters of the Third Kind* and *E.T.,* among many other great movies, today cites that childhood adventure with his father as "my first conscious catharsis."

An entire generation of movie fans can be thankful for the night Mr. Spielberg took his son on a mysterious trip into the desert, because it obviously triggered one of the great creative minds of our time. When Steven Spielberg flexes his imagination, people stand back in awe, but it wasn't always that way for him. Wiels grew up in a middle-class family that broke up when he was in high school. But instead of going off in a corner and crying about his circumstances, he dealt with those difficult circumstances by living out of his imagination.

Wiels used his imagination to get past his family challenges and also his challenges at school, where some tough guys had been picking on him. Guess who the stars of his earliest homemade movies were? The bullies. Suddenly, instead of being beat up by them, Wiels was telling them where to stand, what to say, and how to act. Now, that shows the power of his imagination. Suddenly, the kind of kids who had been picking on him were begging Wiels to let them be involved in his next movie project. So, tell me, is there power in using your imagination or not? Of course there is!

Imagining a Way Out

I played a major role in a little-known movie that Wiels made a few years ago—a film that the public will never see if he wants to remain healthy and on my holiday gift list. Spielberg made the film on a fishing trip that we took with the actor Richard Dreyfuss and a number of other entertainment industry figures who will go nameless because I want to get a few gifts myself.

The fishing trip was waylaid early in the voyage when our chartered boat hit rough water. You can guess what happened to the Hollywood landlubbers on board. It was not our finest hour, but Wiels insisted on capturing it all on camera. I remember him hovering over me at one particularly wretched moment and giving me direction: "Okay, Jake, let the Puke Monster jump on you."

Unlike most great actors, I resisted the director's manipulations. I fought the monster back, but I can't say the same for the rest of our motley crew. A few weeks after this ill-fated voyage, Wiels invited us all over to his house for a special screening of his new limited-run film.

Jaws it wasn't. But once again, Wiels had used his imagination to rise above his circumstances. While the other guys—but not your author—were seriously sick at sea, Wiels tapped into his imagination and escaped seasickness by filming one of the least appealing oceangoing travel documentaries in film history.

Wiels didn't get sick at sea. He got creative. That's not a bad way to handle life when the waters get rough and the sailing isn't so smooth. At one point or another, all of us reach a point where we feel overwhelmed by life. We all experience times when we feel stuck in a bad situation and can't see a way out. Whether it is a job that is driving you crazy, a relationship that isn't working, or money troubles that you can't seem to get a handle on, the key to finding a positive solution is to tap into your imagination and creativity.

Blinded by the Storm

Some of the most challenging and difficult times I can remember were those in which I was *unable* to tap into my imagination and see a way out. When our second child, my son, Nicky, was born, he was five weeks premature and he gave us a real scare. Normally, I'm pretty good in tense situations, but this was my son and when a doctor came out of the newborn examining room and said that Nicky was having breathing difficulties, I locked up. Through the window, I could see him in the incubator with patches on his eyes and tubes in his arms. He weighed only five pounds and looked so small, particularly when I compared him with our daughter, Morgan, who had been born full-term and was nearly twice Nicky's weight.

I was scared out of my wits, and when I brought my wife, Tracey, home from the hospital without Nicky because the doctors wanted to monitor his condition for a few more days, we were both wrecks. The problem was that we were exhausted and scared and we weren't able to look ahead and see Nicky as he is today: a big, strapping three-year-old.

It is tough in those crisis situations to tap into your imagination. I'm not saying you shouldn't deal with the reality of the moment in such challenging times, but at the very least, when you hit rough water, you can use your imagination to peer ahead to better days and calm yourself so that you can better handle the hard times.

The same holds true for plotting your course to a better life. You can use your imagination to map out that path. Even in times when you cannot immediately control what is happening in your life, you still have the power to control your thoughts. If you tap into your imagination, you can create a new reality.

Reel Dreams

I don't think you should ever limit your dreams or your imagination, though you do have to be realistic. I know I am never going to beat out Harrison Ford or Al Pacino as a leading man in Hollywood. I would never be comfortable in that role anyway, since I know casting me in that spot would turn any drama into a comedy immediately. The idea is to use your imagination and visualize new levels of achievement that are just at the *edge of fantasy* but still in the *realm of possibility.*

If you are going to make a mistake, it's far better to dream big than not to dream at all, but you should dream big within your realm of possibility. As I noted earlier, your dreams are the doors to achievement and your imagination is what turns the knob.

I have found my imagination to be a very useful tool. Every day I consciously tap into my imagination to paint a picture of what I want for my family and for my businesses. Then, I hang that picture up in both my conscious and unconscious minds and go to work on making it happen.

Flexing your imagination is nothing new or mysterious. It's often more commonly known as visualization. The practice of visualization is based on the belief that before you create something *physically,* you first create it *mentally.* Most people use visualization unconsciously in their daily lives. Anyone who has ever rearranged furniture, redecorated a room, or restored an old car has started the process by visualizing what the finished product will look like and how the project will be undertaken step by step. Tell me that when you go to the clothing store, you don't decide what to buy by first visualizing yourself in the clothes. See? You, too, are a visualizer.

As an unconscious tool, visualization is useful, but when you train yourself to use it consciously, it can be one of the most effective ways to flex your imagination and write your own life story. Before you can create something better for your life, you first have to imagine it. The great writer Joseph Conrad recognized this when he noted that "imagination, not invention, is the supreme master of art, as of life."

Did you like that? Here's another from my old weight-lifting buddy Ralph Waldo Emerson: "What is the imagination? Only an arm or weapon of the interior energy; only the precursor of the reason."

Getting a Great Visual

Old Ralph Waldo sounds a bit like Obi-Wan Kenobi from *Star Wars,* and why not? Your imagination is the force within you. It is a tool for focusing your interior energy and creating your reality. Visualization is the way you tune in to that inner power. Long before I ever flexed a muscle as a bodybuilder, I was a fanatic about exercising my imagination through visualization. Whether mowing the yard or shooting baskets, I was always visualizing myself doing great things.

When I started lifting weights and really got into bodybuilding, I used my imagination to visualize myself standing on stage competing against the greatest bodybuilders in the world. I'd see myself pumped up, every muscle a work of art, as I competed against all the monstrous guys I saw in those muscle magazines.

I'd be in front of the judges, nailing every pose, making their eyes pop out with my perfectly defined lats, biceps, triceps, calves, thighs, and glutes. I built my body up first in my imagination and later in reality (okay, except for my calves).

I still use visualization in almost every aspect of my life, and I probably do it nearly every day of my life. Every morning while I am working out, I visualize myself accomplishing goals and then going beyond those goals. I tell myself that if I do a thousand sit-ups, I will accomplish all of my goals for the day. Visualization is a way of conditioning myself to break through barriers, just as Roger Bannister did when he broke the four-minute mile.

I use visualization when I sell our Body by Jake fitness equipment on the Home Shopping Network. When doing those shows, I encourage viewers to visualize themselves being more energetic and confident and happier, and I tell them to lock that image into their brains and imagine how it would *feel* to be that way.

I'm only telling my viewers to do what many great athletes have done for years. Football quarterbacks, basketball players, volleyball players, and other athletes—men and women—often talk about using visualization as a tool to prepare for games and as a weapon on the field. Studies have shown that quarterbacks in particular use visualization *during* the game. A quarterback will see a receiver going downfield and will visualize him making a cut and catching the ball in the split second before the quarterback actually throws it.

There has been a great deal of scientific research in the last twenty years on the value of tapping into the imagination as a method for enhancing peak performance. Scientists say that this inner power may well be the most important resource that we have. No less an intellectual giant than Albert Einstein once noted, "Imagination is more important than knowledge." There are hundreds of books on the power of the mind, and many serious scientists and psychologists have studied and written about the use of imagination in guiding your life. They call it *neurolinguistic programming* and *self-talk*.

Of course, modern-day scientists are only rediscovering something that others have known for hundreds and hundreds of years. In the Bible's Book of Proverbs is the message "Without a vision, the people perish." This vision stuff is not New Age. The power of imagination is an incredible and time-proven tool that can help you take your dreams and plant them in your heart and mind.

Visualization can help you determine what you need to do to prepare yourself for the type of success you dream of. When I became hooked on working out back in my basement bedroom in Long Island, one of the ways I motivated myself was to look in that skinny mirror on my bedroom door and envision myself with muscles like my boyhood hero Charles Bronson.

Try it now by going off on your own. Find some quiet place away from the radio, television, and any other distractions, and follow these steps.

1. Relax yourself mentally and physically by clearing your mind and by taking deep breaths. Let go of all those things from your past that may be holding you back. Did somebody hurt your feelings? Get over it. Did you make a mistake or fail at something you tried? So what? Here is a way to handle things that happened to you in the past: *You are no longer the person you were then, so what happened then should not hold you back now.*

2. Visualize the life you want for yourself now. See yourself working happily in your dream job. Picture yourself in the relationship you want, living where you want, doing what you want, going after what you want. Don't ask why you should not have these things. Instead, take ownership of them. Believe that you have every right to go after what you want.

3. Now color in the details. When my daughter, Morgan, who is a very artistic five-year-old (if I do say so myself), draws a picture, she doesn't consider it complete until she has colored in every detail with her crayons. You should be equally thorough in visualizing yourself pursuing your goals and achieving them. Color in all the details so that you get a real sense of what it will feel like to be living exactly the life you want to live. Once you've got a really vivid picture in your mind, you will be ready to follow your imagination wherever it takes you. See yourself traveling from where you are now to where you want to be. Envision the journey step by step.

4. Spend some extended time basking in the emotions that you imagine you would feel if you were living that dream. How would it feel to be in that relationship, in that job, in that situation you dream of? Capture this feeling in your emotional memory so that you can summon it up and feel it when you are going after your goals and dreams.

5. Think about your dreams of success, the things you want to do with your life, and then ask yourself what you need to do to be prepared for that success. Do you need more education? Do you need more experience? Do you need to get in better physical shape? Are there challenges in your personal life that you need to resolve? Bad habits that you need to kick? Better habits that you need to establish?

6. Finally, take time every day to visualize yourself going after your dreams, and then think about what you need to do to get on track.

If you are having trouble tuning in to that vision, try this: Think of climbing a mountain. Envision yourself preparing for the climb. What equipment do you have in that vision? What training? What attitude? What physical condition are you in? Who is with you? What sort of help are they providing you? What kind of people are they? What things have you left at home in order to make this climb? What people have you left behind because they were more likely to be a hindrance?

Now, apply the same thought processes to your dreams for your career or your relationships or your life in general. Ask yourself the same questions, and write down your answers. Do you see the value of visualization?

Write Your Own Story and Live It

Remember when I noted earlier that the successful people I trained are determined to write their own life stories? Well, you use your imagination and visualization to write the first draft. Then you spend the rest of your life turning it into a masterpiece.

All of the successful people I know use visualization in their lives in one form or another. All of them use their imagination to create a larger vision of what they want to do and where they want to go. I also know a lot of people who don't do it. You see them all the time, people who seem never to have gotten beyond a certain level. I see them in the gym where I work out. There are men and women for whom having the perfect physique is the ultimate dream. You have to give them credit. They work hard at that dream. They make sacrifices. They stay with it. A lot of them keep pushing to get bigger and bigger so that when they strut down the street in extra-small T-shirts and short shorts, traffic stops.

The problem is, their vision is too limited. I'm not saying every-one has to want to do what I do, or that I am any smarter or bet-ter. But a lot of those bodybuilders in the gym barely get by financially, when the fact is they could have more well-rounded and successful lives if they used their imagination and applied that same determination and drive to create a greater vision.

My late grandma Myra Duberstein, whom you will be reading a lot about in this book, must have worried that I would never ex-pand my vision, because when I was a teenager working out with weights and reading muscle magazines all the time, she'd shake her finger at me and say, "If you spent as much time reading good books as you spend working out, you would be another Einstein!"

She saw that I had plenty of energy and focus when I was involved in something that was compatible with my goals, but she worried that my goals were too limited, and she was right. It wasn't until I removed those limitations that I really began to achieve fantastic things. Those people who never leave the gym have limited their vision. For them, lifting a certain weight or reaching a physical goal is the Ultimate Goal. I understand that, because that was the way I thought at one point. But when I began training some of the most successful men and women in show business, my vision expanded. I let my imagination run wild. I realized that weight training was not the Ultimate Goal. It was something that I loved to do, it made me feel great. But it was only a means to an end. It helped me reach the next level. I used my imagination to decide what that level would be. You can do it, too!

POWERLIVING
LESSON NO. 3

Go for the Goal

I was standing in my underwear in the freezing cold with a stick in my hand on the Syracuse University lacrosse field in frigid upstate New York when it hit me.

What the heck am I doing with my life?

I wasn't really in my underwear. I was wearing a mesh jersey and uniform shorts for the Cortland State University lacrosse team. We were playing Syracuse in a scrimmage in the snow. It was March, but there was a minus-20 wind-chill factor. I was a freshman at Cortland State. My grades were mediocre and I didn't particularly care. I had enrolled in college to please my parents. It was their goal, not mine. It wasn't that I didn't think getting an education was a good idea. It was just that I didn't know what kind of education I wanted. I had friends and roommates who had come to college with goals. They wanted to be botanists or chemists, lawyers or businesspeople, and so they were motivated to take classes in botany, chemistry, law, and business. I didn't know what I wanted to do. I was *there,* but I wasn't going anywhere.

If this had been a science-fiction movie, the guys in the white coats would have taken one look and declared that freshman Jake Steinfeld was in a state of "suspended education." I was hanging around and I had a pulse, but there were few signs of actual brain activity. I knew I was lucky even to be on campus. Without any real plans for my life, I hadn't applied myself much in high school and I hadn't scored high enough on the college entrance exams to be accepted on that basis. But Cortland had an alumni admission program in which they admitted a few students who didn't meet academic standards but showed potential because of their leadership abilities or unique talents.

To get in under this special admissions program was tough. There were only a few slots, so there was a lot of competition. You had to impress a committee of faculty members and alumni in an interview. My high school guidance counselor, Tommy Lamandola, who was also a bodybuilder and had been a role model for me, recommended me to the special admissions committee at Cortland. He believed in me and he helped psych me up for the interview. My father also motivated me with a negative psych-up: "You have an opportunity here to win them over with your personality, since you obviously can't do it with your grades."

Mr. Entertainment

The pressure was on to impress the committee. I wasn't much at calculus, but I was already a pretty good salesman. I had yet to learn about dressing for success, though. I was seventeen years old and I had only one suit. It was a green corduroy ensemble, just the right outfit for a hot and humid summer day—not to mention a high-pressure, do-or-die meeting with the admissions committee.

When we drove onto the campus, I ducked down in the backseat so nobody would see me in that ugly suit. We parked and went to the administration building, where we were directed to have a seat in the lobby outside the office of the dean of admissions. I decided I was going to have to do this in my own way. I was still stuttering some, but I'd been working out for a couple of years by then, and my self-confidence was up. I tapped into my imagination and decided that this was Las Vegas, the admissions committee were the audience, and I was Mr. Entertainment.

When they called me in, I walked around the room, introducing myself, shaking hands, making eye contact. I was imitating my grandmother the irrepressible Mrs. Myra Duberstein, who was a genius at turning strangers into bosom buddies. She had trained me how to work a crowd, and she had trained me well. "How ya doin'? I'm Jake Steinfeld, pleased to meetcha."

When the formal interview began, we sat down around a table the size of Long Island. They explained the program to me, and told me that there were nearly a hundred other applicants—just to let me know how high the stakes were. Then, it was my turn.

I opened with a joke, and most of them smiled, although a few looked a little stunned. Then I went into my pitch: "I think I can make Cortland State a better place. I like people. I am a hard worker and now that I've learned how to build my body, I think I can apply it to my studies. What can I say? I'm a late bloomer, but I think Cortland State can really help me grow and flourish. I'm willing to work hard if you give me the chance."

To my absolute amazement, they bought it. The committee was all smiles when they sent me out the door and told me I'd definitely be hearing from them. A few weeks later, I got the acceptance notice in the mail. I wasn't sure whether to be happy or to cry. I didn't have a clue what I was going to study. The admissions counselor took care of my lack of goals by putting me in General Studies until I could figure out what I wanted to do with myself in the classroom. I had no problem keeping busy elsewhere.

The Young and the Clueless

Along with making the lacrosse team, I was nominated by my buddies to run for president of Higgins Hall, my dorm, and I was the only freshman on campus to get a job in the hottest disco in town—and the only disco in town: the Shamrock. The run at the dorm presidency went down the tubes shortly after the first semester, though. We needed to raise some "soft money" for my dorm presidency campaign, so I organized a "Las Vegas night" with crap tables, blackjack, roulette, the whole Casino Royale treatment.

Originally, we planned it as sort of a low-key, behind-closed-doors thing just for the guys in the dorm, the lacrosse team, and a few other select people. But word got around, and on the designated night there were 450 people lined up to get in before we even started to roll the dice. The dorm manager sent everybody home and the presidential candidate was sent to his room. I told them, "Hey, you admitted me because I promised to bring something unique to the university. Now you're gonna be mad at me for doing it?"

Okay, so I was the most clueless and goalless guy on campus. It finally struck me as I stood on the field at Syracuse freezing my buttissimo off and wondering what the heck I was doing with my life. It hit me like a forearm to the chin; in fact, it may well have been some Syracuse player's actual forearm to my chin that jolted my brain and woke me up. Suddenly, I realized I wasn't really goalless, I just had gotten waylaid while trying to please my folks. I thought, "I'm wasting my time and my parents' money here. I'm 'retiring' from school and moving to L.A. to be a bodybuilder. That's what I really want to do. *That's* my goal!"

It had been my dream ever since that first weight-training session with Sinatra and our fans in my basement. Now, after screwing around at college for a few months, I felt it was what I *had* to do. It wasn't exactly a decision to run for Congress or to save the world from the threat of nuclear war, but it was my own humble dream at the time and I went after it.

Running into a Wall on First and Goal

It was such an exciting feeling to finally have my own goal. Of course, when I called my mother to tell her, she dropped the phone like it had turned into a rattlesnake. At first I thought she had fainted, but then she began yelling for my father: "Herbie, come talk to your son. I'm putting my head in the oven."

I'll never forget the trip home to face them with this decision for the first time. I was scared to death that they would try to stop me, and, to tell you the truth, scared that they might *not* try to stop me.

This decision was definitely what I wanted, but it was a big step. I didn't have any money or a car, and I didn't know anybody in L.A. This was a big leap for me, but I felt it was one I had to make.

I still felt guilty, though. Here I was, the oldest child, who was expected to get an education and to elevate the family name. There was a lot of competition among my parents and their friends as far as how their kids were doing. The other offspring were mostly well on their way to careers in law, medicine, or junk-bond trading. I could hear the conversation at the mah-jongg party coming to a dead halt when my mother's turn came to brag about her son: "Oh, our boy Jake? Well, he is a physiology self-constructor. He builds his body, and he has pectorals to die for!"

Needless to say, my parents took a lot of convincing when I said I wanted to abandon higher education for bodybuilding, but in the end, I have to give them credit; they treated me like the adult that I wasn't. They saw that this was what I really wanted to do. They understood that even if I was making a huge mistake, it was a lesson I had to learn for myself.

Looking back now as a parent myself, I understand that they thought the traditional route through college was the best thing for me. They didn't see any future in bodybuilding because in their world it didn't exist. I certainly didn't foresee that *I* would be the guy to create personal fitness training. So I couldn't expect my parents to foresee it.

They probably envisioned me in the future as a sun-dried fifty-year-old muscle head standing on the Santa Monica Pier with a tin cup: "Hey, mistah, I'll flex my biceps for a buck!"

In the end, though, my folks came through. They helped me lease a 1977 Chevy Camaro and gave me enough money to get an apartment and find a job. "Go out there, and whenever you are ready to come back home we will be here," my mother said, although I could tell she was afraid I was off on a wild-goose chase.

Maybe, when all was said and done, my parents realized that it was far better to let me direct all of my energy to chasing a dream than for me to be wandering around without a clue, getting into hot water because I had too much energy to burn. They were right. I was about to discover one of the most valuable things about having goals: Even if they turn out to be the wrong goals, they put you on the right road, the road to self-determination.

Taking Control

Read the sentences below. Do any of them sound familiar?

- They are always making me do things I don't want to do.
- Why do things like this always happen to me?
- I've had so many interruptions today, I haven't gotten anything done.
- I'd love to get more education, but there are just too many other things I have to do.
- I know I'm always late, but whenever I try to do anything, something always happens to me.

These are typical laments for a person without a goal. What is common to each of them? There is always someone, or something, else to blame for the person's circumstances. The reality, of course, is that until *you* make the conscious decision to take responsibility for writing your own life's story, you have nobody to blame but yourself for circumstances that you don't like.

If you are unhappy in your job or your relationship, it is your responsibility to set new goals and go after them. If you don't have goals, you live without focus, and you will eventually find yourself in circumstances like mine: standing out in the cold in my underwear, wondering what the heck was happening with my life. If you listen to your dreams and set goals based on them, you stop the drifting. People without goals wander aimlessly and without direction. Those with clear goals are in the greatest chase of all, the relentless pursuit of happiness and fulfillment called PowerLiving.

When do you most enjoy your life? When do you get so lost in what you are doing that you don't notice anything else going on around you and you lose all track of time? For most people, this pleasurable feeling occurs when they are engaged in an activity with well-defined goals, whether it is playing a game of basketball, being engrossed in a game of chess, or becoming absorbed in reading a book, writing an essay, or redecorating a room. Human beings are wired for goals. Without them, we flounder around. A life without goals is a life without purpose or direction.

How many times have you set out on a trip without first deciding where it is you want to go? Why would you do that? What is the purpose of a trip with no destination? How will you know when you have arrived if you don't know where you are going?

The same holds true in life. When you have identified someplace that you really want to go in life, some goal you want to achieve, then you are less inclined to waste time or to be distracted—or to waste your creativity and energy on things like Las Vegas nights in your college dormitory (although there's nothing wrong with a little fun now and then).

When you have a series of smaller goals that build to more meaningful higher goals and an Ultimate Goal, the journey becomes the thing. Suddenly, you are no longer letting life act on you. You are acting on it. You are actively involved in creating your own destiny. Goals are crucial to PowerLiving. They are vital. They are the only way to fly.

Once you have learned to use your imagination as a tool, you are ready to turn your dreams into concrete goals. This is a major step because goals are your dreams translated into reality.

Building Brain Bridges

Some people have trouble setting goals because it involves switching from one side of the brain to the other. You dream with the right side of your brain, which houses your creative powers. This is the most active part of the brain for artists, writers, actors, and other highly creative people. Think of this as the Robin Williams side of your brain.

The left side of your brain is home to your logical and analytical functions. This is where you go to do algebra, figure your taxes, and to write computer software programs. Think of this as the Bill Gates side of your brain.

Now, I can't say for certain, but my guess is that Robin Williams, who is probably the world's most wildly creative comedian, would be helpless if you asked him to audit your taxes. I would also be willing to bet you a couple of carrot juice shakes that Microsoft CEO Bill Gates doesn't entertain his shareholders for hours and hours with hilarious stories about how he and a buddy developed the world's most widely used computer operating system.

I'm not saying Gates isn't creative, mind you, or that Robin doesn't use logic in his comedy. But they, like most of us, favor one side of the brain or the other, and it can be difficult to cross over. Setting goals is one of those things that require you to bridge the gap between your dreams and your logic. To do it, you have to translate your dreams into reality by transferring them from your imagination into action. If you're having trouble understanding this, think about another brain-bridging activity, writing.

When you take something that you have been thinking about and write it down, you are translating a thought into action, which is exactly what you do when you create goals. Take time now to write down your goals, following these five steps.

1. Find a quiet place. Get comfortable. Relax. Clear all the clutter out of your mind and focus on what you want more than anything else.

   This is the stage in which you tap into your imagination. A lot of people are like I was. I had a goal for a long time but I didn't realize it. Maybe, like some, I thought there was something *mystical* about having a goal. Some people seem to think that you have to be like Moses and go to the mountaintop to pick up your goals from some divine delivery service. It doesn't happen that way, unless you're Charlton Heston.

   Goals are pretty simple to find once you tap into your imagination. What do most people want in life? They want to be happy. If they are reasonable people, they don't expect to be happy all the time, but it's something to shoot for. So, what makes you happy? Okay, sure, eating chocolate cake makes you happy; there are a lot of things that make you happy. But what is it that makes you happy that you can make a living from? What can you do over the course of an entire lifetime to feel fulfilled and maybe contribute to the betterment of the world around you, too? Ahh, that's a little more difficult. But it's still not that difficult.

There is another factor to add into this goal-defining process. What is it that makes you happy that allows you to use your natural talents and gifts and intelligence to the fullest extent? Usually they go hand in hand. Most people are happy doing what they do best, whether it's being involved in sports, caring for others, teaching, writing, or running a business that creates jobs and wealth for a community.

2. Test-drive your goal.

Before you take the first steps toward your goal, use your imagination to take it for a test drive. Envision yourself going after this goal and consider whether you are willing to make the sacrifices and changes that may be necessary to attain the goal. If you have doubts that the goal is worth it, or that it is a good fit, then it probably isn't. Most goals, particularly your Ultimate Goal, come with a certificate of certainty attached: "Yes, this is what I want, without a doubt." If that is how you feel about your goal, then it is almost certainly the right one for you.

The next step in your goal test drive is to ask yourself, "What is the worst that could happen if I go after this goal and give it all I've got, but don't achieve it?" Most of the time, the worst that can happen when you pursue a goal is ten times better than the *best* that could happen if you don't pursue any goals at all.

I'll show you an example of this in my own life later in the book, but for now consider the young actress who dreams of being a leading lady. As her career progresses from acting student to minor stage roles and then to starring roles, she realizes after several years that there are few good roles for leading ladies and that the actresses who get those roles tend to have short careers. She yearns for more challenging work. Then she meets a great character actress in her seventies who tells her of the wonderful and fulfilling life she has had playing a wide variety of roles on stage, on television, and in the movies. This veteran character actress has had steady and rewarding work all of her life and she still loves it. The young actress decides she is going to model her career on that of the character actress, and after adjusting her goals, she enjoys her career more than ever before.

The young actress had to abandon her original goal when she saw that it was not giving her fulfillment, but because she was chasing a goal, her life had so much momentum that she immediately found a more suitable path. If she had not been in pursuit of a goal in the first place, she never would have found that more fulfilling option. You have to get in the game by selecting goals and going after them, so that your life takes on momentum.

Remember that word, "momentum." It is from the Latin *movere,* "to move." If you are going to get your life moving, you need to build momentum by setting goals and going after them. Like the woman in the example above, and like many, many other people, you may have to adjust your goals as you go. But if you build up momentum, you create the power to build a *momentous* life—a life of significance, accomplishment, and fulfillment—no matter what your Ultimate Goal eventually becomes.

Once again, the important thing is to be in the game, pursuing a goal, writing your own life story. For now, understand that if you are truly pursuing a goal that has meaning for you, in the end it won't matter if you don't get *exactly* what you set out for because as you make the journey, you will change, and your goals may change, too.

3. Now, write down your goal. Or draw a picture or create a symbol of it in a notebook, in a personal journal, or simply on a piece of paper.

I've found that it is extremely helpful to write down my goals because just the act of writing them down makes them seem doable. It gets me focused and motivated to see well-defined goals on paper. When you write down your goals, you are taking an important step, you are writing the outline for your own life story. And when you do that, it means you are no longer willing to let outside events or other people dictate how you live your life. You are practicing PowerLiving.

It also doesn't hurt to occasionally read your goal out loud. Say, "I am going to do this, no matter what! I am a winner! I will not quit!" Every time you write down your goals, read them, and say them out loud, you transfer them from your creative consciousness to your logical consciousness and you reinforce the fact in your mind that they are real and that they are achievable.

4. Now envision yourself accomplishing the goal, being on top of the mountain. Bask in it. Feel the satisfaction and pride it will bring you. Smell it, touch it, taste it. Get all of your senses involved in the pleasure of it. Envision yourself on track to your goal in six months, a year, five years, ten years, twenty years. See yourself near the end of your life and feel the satisfaction that comes from PowerLiving. Get a sense of what it would be like to know that you have put your talents, your brains, all of your gifts and resources to their highest use in living your life.

5. Finally, write down what it was like to *feel* the accomplishment; then, note any images that come into your mind regarding things you can do, steps you can take to go after your goal.

Take all the time you need to fully explore this, and once you have written down the feelings and savored them, put the things you have written in a safe place where you can pull them out and go over them regularly. When times get challenging, and they will, it can be extremely helpful to go over this material and to recharge your batteries emotionally and physically by reading what motivated you to set these goals in the first place.

Try to do these five steps at least once a day, especially when you are starting out, and then run through them again whenever you feel you need more motivation.

You'll find it helps you stay on the path and in control.

Keep Your Eyes on the Prize

Think again about going on that mountain-climbing adventure that I referred to in the previous chapter. What motivates you more, visualizing yourself at the bottom of the mountain looking up at where you have to go—or standing at the top of the mountain looking down at what you have accomplished?

For most people, it works best to envision yourself having accomplished the goal and to think of all the benefits and rewards this will bring. Then, with that image in mind, you will be focused and motivated to set out on that path step by step. You never know what will happen once you get on that path, but *it is far better to be on a path of your choosing than on one chosen by someone else.*

The H-Man

Recently I saw a magazine story entitled "Your Everyday, Down-to-Earth, Run-of-the-Mill $20 Million Star." I didn't have to read it to know whom it was about: Harrison Ford, or, as I call him, "the H-Man." Whenever I get to thinking about what a messed-up kid *I* was, I comfort myself by thinking about Harrison as a kid. He was no young Indiana Jones.

Here is a guy who belonged to both the model railroad club and the social science club at Park Ridge High School in Chicago. This suave leading man who has saved not only the world but the entire galaxy numerous times in his movie roles was an audiovisual assistant in high school. His job was to wheel overhead projectors up and down the hall. Like me, Harrison was one of the young and the goalless in college. He was thrown out of Ripon College in Wisconsin for what he now describes as "total academic failure." Harrison had taken some acting courses before being booted out of college, and so he moved to California to try acting. In his first role, he played a bellhop and appeared in the movie just long enough to hand James Coburn a telegram.

At one point, Harrison found himself standing out in the cold with only some bit acting parts to his credit, two kids, and a handful of unpaid bills. There is nothing like financial pressure and a family to focus you on setting some serious goals. One thing you can say about Harrison is that he is a determined and resourceful guy. "They tried to kill me off with poisons, sharp sticks, and blunt objects, but I was like a snake that grew a new tail," he said of those days in an interview.

To pay the bills for his growing family, he went to the library, read everything he could on carpentry, and soon had a whole new career going as a Hollywood handyman. He built a recording studio for the musician Sergio Mendes, a sundeck for Sally Kellerman, and bookcases for the authors John Gregory Dunne and Joan Didion. If I was "the fitness guru to the stars," Harrison was "carpenter to the stars."

When Steven Spielberg took me along during the filming of *Indiana Jones and the Temple of Doom,* I trained Harrison too. I had a lot of fun with him because he is such a no-nonsense, intense guy. I'd get him doing push-ups while I counted them off, and I'd slowly pick up the pace until he'd give me one of his patented glares. But he would keep pushing. That is where we invented silent training camp. He'd give me a look that said, "Hey, pal, I can count too."

Harrison does not believe in hype. He believes that if you work hard, you make your own luck. "I've had scientifically provable luck from time to time. Being in the right place at the right time and then doing the right thing. You cannot get where I got without luck," he said in an interview once.

He may talk about being lucky, but Harrison is without a doubt one of the most focused and goal-oriented people I've ever known. Believe me, he is a driven man, although he can be a lot of fun, too, and don't ever let him catch you trying to one-up him. I know from experience what he will do to put you in your place.

After one long hot day of filming on location in London, Harrison threw his Indiana Jones fedora into the trunk of his car and asked me if I wanted to ride back to the hotel with him. On the way, he suggested we stop at a pub for a beer. I thought it would be fun to see how the Brits in the pub responded to a movie star in their midst. When we walked into the packed pub, the patrons all looked up immediately, but it wasn't Harrison they were staring at, it was *me*. In fact, they surrounded me, and one little guy spoke up. "Aren't you an American footballer?" he said.

I'd forgotten all about it, but the big thing going on that weekend in London was a preseason exhibition football game between two NFL teams at Wembley Stadium. It was the first time American football had been played in London. The chaps in the pub had mistaken me for one of the professional football players, and I was only too happy to play the role while Mr. Movie Star was ignored.

"Why, yes, I'm one of the American footballers," I told the boys in the pub. "Let me buy a round of drinks for everyone."

As I prepared to thrill my English fans with stories of my athletic exploits, I turned around to make sure that Harrison was paying attention. He was nowhere to be seen, so I figured he'd ditched me. But then, out of the corner of my eye, I saw a figure standing near the door.

It was Harrison in his Indiana Jones hat, wooing the lassies and wowing the laddies. I had eight drinks in my arms for my fans, but there was nobody standing around me. As they surrounded him, Harrison looked at me with a gleam of total victory in his eyes. The cinematic hero sticking it to the football phony. Like I said: Nobody upstages Harrison Ford.

Goals Are Opportunity Magnets

It was a great retaliatory move on Harrison's part, and the sort of thing I have come to expect from him. One reason we get along so well is that we both have had to work hard for what we have accomplished. Like me, Harrison understands the importance of setting goals. His success serves also as an example of the fact that when you set goals for your life and keep after them, you create a positive energy that draws people, and opportunity, to you.

Think a second about someone you know who has no goals, someone who doesn't seem to care about bettering himself or herself. Do you feel like reaching out to that person and helping? Not if the person isn't trying to do anything on her own. But when people see that you are working on a dream, they are drawn to lend a hand. Even if you are struggling and fighting to keep it alive, people admire that. They want to invest in your dream because you obviously believe in yourself.

Now that I have two kids, I've realized that adults sometimes forget things that came naturally to them as children. I watch Morgan and Nicky set goals all the time. They decide what they want and they could care less about *how* they are going to get it. They just go after it relentlessly. They lock their goals in and then keep after them until they accomplish the mission. This is how it starts as soon as we sit down to dinner.

"Daddy and Mommy, can we watch a video tonight?"

"We'll see how well you eat."

Two bites later.

"Can we watch a video after dinner? I really want to watch a video. Which video can we watch? Can we watch two?"

Kids are *relentless* in going after what they want. They never take their eyes off the goal. If one approach doesn't work, they'll try another and another, and if you let them, they will wear you out. Why is it that as adults, we often lose that dedication to our goals? Why are we so easily knocked off track? When many people set goals, they can't seem to get past worrying about the *how*. They don't understand, as children seem to, that they should just keep after what they want and let the *how* take care of itself.

Now, that's not to say you shouldn't have a plan for going after your goals. In fact, that is what the next chapter is about. But some people become so obsessed with worrying about what *might* happen or the challenges they *might* encounter that they can't see far enough ahead even to draw up a plan. When you create goals built from your dreams, the *how* will come to you over time.

The Ultimate Goal

Keep in mind that you can and should have more than one goal. Most people have what I call an Ultimate Goal. Your Ultimate Goal is the beacon for everything you do, every day of your journey. Like the small-plane pilot who adjusts his course to a signal transmitted from his destination airport, you determine whether you are on course by checking whether your actions are in alignment with your Ultimate Goal. This goal is like the sun in your personal universe. All of your other goals revolve around it. It defines them and it defines your life, just as the power of the sun provides the light, heat, and energy that define our world.

Historians note that most civilizations have been guided by their Ultimate Goals. In ancient Greece, it was thought that heroic deeds would guarantee passage into a higher kingdom upon death, and so the Greeks built their entire civilization upon the need to do heroic things. It was their Ultimate Goal. It gave meaning to their daily existence.

Unlike lesser goals, your Ultimate Goal encompasses more than self-interest, and often, it grows as you grow. When I was nineteen years old, I would have said my Ultimate Goal was to be Mr. America. Today, I realize that is far too narrow for an Ultimate Goal, which is something you strive for over an entire lifetime. Now, I would say my Ultimate Goal is to create a rewarding and fulfilling life for not only myself but my entire family and all those I care about.

This goal requires that every decision I make be evaluated not only in terms of my self-interest ("Will it be good for my career? Is it a good investment for me? How will this impact me?") but also in terms of the well-being of Tracey, Morgan, Nicky, and the others who depend on me to look out for them.

With an Ultimate Goal that encompasses the interests of the people who matter to me, I have guidelines for selecting my other goals. Earlier in my life, before I had my own family, my Ultimate Goal was more narrow in scope. At that point I was focused on becoming an entrepreneur in the health and fitness field. Inspired in part by what I had seen Ted Turner create when I was doing my fitness breaks on CNN, my Ultimate Goal was to have a multifaceted multimedia company. That was what I measured every move against. I had completed four hundred episodes of my half-hour fitness show and my contract was up for renewal when I decided it was time to make a major move. I had a new contract on my desk that called for two more years on ESPN. It was a very lucrative deal, but it didn't measure up to my Ultimate Goal. What I really wanted to do at that point was create my own twenty-four-hour cable network, just as Ted Turner had done, only mine would be built around fitness and health.

Before I jumped back on ESPN, I wanted to run my idea about a new network past someone who knew the cable industry. I had the perfect guy. During this same period, I'd been doing the half-hour sitcom *Big Brother Jake* on the Family Channel. The president and CEO of that cable network was Tim Robertson, a first-class guy whom I had grown to respect and trust.

I went to Tim with the idea, telling him that it was part of my Ultimate Goal. He bought in to it. In fact, International Family Entertainment became my partner in what was originally known as the Cable Health Club but is now called FiT TV. Today our programming reaches nearly 15 million homes and FiT TV is a key part of my multifaceted multimedia business enterprise.

Zigzagging Through Life

When you always keep a picture of your Ultimate Goal in your mind, every day of your life takes on a purpose, and when you become that focused, the *how* will come to you. In the beginning you don't need to know the route, you don't even need to know how to get there. You need only to stay close, and to remain focused on that final destination, your Ultimate Goal.

Chances are you will not find a direct route straight to every one of your smaller goals—few people do. The important thing is always to *stay close* to them while always staying in alignment with your Ultimate Goal. Most of us have to work our way toward our Ultimate Goal by setting smaller goals that keep us in the ballpark. I know of a guy who dreamed of being a recording-studio engineer. He even paid a lot of money and spent several extra years in college to get a degree in acoustical engineering. But the only job he could get out of college was as a janitor at the recording studio of a rock and roll band. He turned it down because he felt he needed a better-paying job right away to pay the debts from his schooling. That guy never made it into the recording industry; he wandered off course and became a computer technician, a perfectly good career too. For the rest of his life, he regretted not taking the janitor's job, because it would have kept him close to his Ultimate Goal.

Nailing a Solo Performance

Do you know what Harrison Ford was doing when he got his biggest break? He was on his knees nailing boards for a new office entrance at Goldwyn Studios in Hollywood. He looked up, and walking toward him were George Lucas and Richard Dreyfuss. Although he felt "like a doofus," Harrison said he couldn't hide. He knew Lucas because he'd had a very small part as a small-town hot-rodder in *American Graffiti,* which Lucas had directed. When Lucas spotted him, he invited Harrison into his office to talk. During the conversation, Lucas mentioned that he was casting a new movie, *Star Wars,* and he invited Harrison to the testing, but only as a stand-in for the other actors to "bounce lines off."

Someone less committed to his goals might have gone back to sawing boards, but Harrison went to the casting sessions, bounced off a bunch of big-name actors, and ended up stealing the starring role of Han Solo—the role that really launched his acting career.

Like many successful people, Harrison had to take a few detours and side roads while pursuing his goal, but he kept his focus. Even when he had a well-defined goal, Harrison didn't have an easy path. He had to deal with rejection and setbacks and hard times just like everybody else. But he understood that the important thing is always to keep that goal locked in your sights. When you set your goals and then go after them, you have to focus on the mountaintop, not the climb, and you should never, ever look down. Always keep your eyes focused ahead, because that is where your Ultimate Goal awaits you!

POWERLIVING
LESSON NO. 4

Get in the Flow!

Tracey and I were sitting in a small theater watching a movie a while back. It seemed like a nice enough film, but I have to admit I was distracted by a somewhat different movie playing out in my head. You are familiar with the plot by now: A fat kid with a speech impediment from a middle-class family in Long Island struggles through high school and never makes it past the first year of college. Having discovered the benefits of bodybuilding, he goes off to L.A. to become Mr. America, but that dream goes bust, so while working two-bit jobs around town, he helps an actress get in shape for a commercial. The next thing he knows, he has created the personal fitness training industry while working with some of the most famous and powerful people in the entertainment industry. These people inspire him to develop his business and his own acting career to heights he never imagined, while continually spinning one success into another.

My movie reaches its dramatic high point when the kid from Long Island, now grown up, finds himself daydreaming in a movie theater inside the White House, sitting directly behind the president of the United States. As the background music reaches a crescendo, the president of the United States, the commander in chief, the leader of the free world, turns back, looks the now grown-up kid in the eye, and says, "Hey, Jake, you don't have *butter* on that popcorn, do you?"

Roll the credits. It's a wrap. What a life! That's PowerLiving!

The story about being in the White House movie theater is true and President Clinton did say that to me.

It is also true that while Tracey and I were supposed to be watching a movie at the White House, I was running the movie of my own life story in my head. As much as the audience enjoyed the official White House film that night, I have no doubt that I enjoyed mine more.

I have had an incredible life so far, and I've only just recently learned to stop every now and then and savor it. When you do that, it gives you an even greater appreciation for the gifts that life has given you—the people you've met, the love you've felt, the luck you've had, the blessings that have come your way. I've come to discover that when I take time to savor my life, I find myself looking forward with even greater enthusiasm to the rest of this journey—every day, every hour, and every minute of it.

The Journey Is the Thing

The really great thing about having goals is not achieving them— it is the *process* that you go through to get there. You have to have a process, or a plan; otherwise, even if you set an Ultimate Goal you won't have any way of getting to it. Having a plan, or a series of smaller goals that progressively lead you to your Ultimate Goal, will not guarantee that you will get exactly what you want in life, but when you have a plan it prepares you for all the opportunities that present themselves along the way. And that is what makes life an adventure, the joy of the journey.

Think about your favorite championship team, whether it is a Little League team you played on or a professional team you root for. Winning that final championship game was great, wasn't it? But the best part is the entire season that led up to it, play by play, game by game, building success upon success. That's where the joy is in sports, and in life too.

The thrill is not so much in claiming the trophy or the prize, it is in all the rewards you experience while getting to the victory stand. What will you remember most about the championship? The trophy? Naw, it'll go on a shelf somewhere. What you remember most is what it took to claim that trophy, all of the hard work, all of the lucky breaks, all of the teamwork and preparation, all of the excitement of PowerLiving during that period of your life.

A Plan Puts Your Life in Play

There is no way I could ever have dreamed of all the great twists and turns my life has taken. I certainly can't say that ten years ago, or even five years ago, I planned out exactly where my life would be today. But I did plan for *success,* and I did prepare myself for the opportunities that put me in a position to be successful.

My original plan was to take my enthusiasm and talent for bodybuilding and become Mr. America. The reality of what has happened has far exceeded that dream, but I have remained in alignment with my Ultimate Goal of providing for my family and building a life in the health and fitness field. None of it would have happened, though, if I had not first had that Ultimate Goal, and then pursued that goal with a plan that, while it changed from time to time, still kept me prepared for and alert to opportunities.

The great thing about having a plan for your life is that once you get it in place, you go from being someone *waiting* for something to happen to being someone who *makes* things happen. When you are determined to make things happen in your life, you prepare yourself for success; then, suddenly, all sorts of unexpected opportunities begin to appear. Having a plan also builds and reinforces an attitude that you are willing to do whatever it takes to make those opportunities work.

Although I am providing you with the tools you will need to go after your dreams, it is up to you to use them. I can guarantee that you will *never* accomplish your dreams and goals if you don't have a plan for going after them. I can also guarantee that whatever it is you want in life will not just come to you. You have to go after it, and you'd better have some sort of plan in place to do that. Without a plan, you can easily lose sight of your Ultimate Goal, just as you can lose your way on a trip if you don't have a map. Without a plan, you can wander off course too easily, get discouraged, and become frustrated. But if you have a goal in mind, and a plan on how to get there, you always know where you are headed.

Homing In on Your Goals

I have a confession to make: My name is Jake, and I am a list addict. I've blown thousands of dollars on Post-it notes over the years. My wife and children hide my lists from me, but to no avail. I write new ones. My list-making impulse hits me every Sunday night. I'll be lying in bed thinking about all I have to get accomplished the next day and week and month and year and millennium . . . and for some reason I start feeling overwhelmed. Can you believe that?

To set my mind, not to mention my poor wife's mind, at rest, I'll get up, go into my office at home, and spend a few minutes— okay, an hour or two—writing down what I have to do just in the week ahead. Then I break it down to what needs to be done each day. Then I divide up each day and assign myself tasks for each morning, afternoon, and night. I prioritize everything. I also make lists of people I have to talk to. No one is safe. And you thought the nightlife in La-La Land was all movie premieres and parties by the pool!

Part of my need to write things down comes from the fact that, like most business entrepreneurs, I like to have a lot of things going all the time. If I were a juggler, I'd have the usual bowling pins, beach balls, and swords up in the air, but I would also have movie scripts, television deals, my own magazine, endorsement contracts, and all sorts of other stuff flying around.

It's all part of my overall plan. I have a lot of energy and I believe in getting a lot of things going because it is inevitable that some things fall through or take longer to unfold than you think—especially when it comes to developing movie and television projects. If you've only got one thing going and it falls through or hits a snag, you're left hanging. But if you keep a lot of things going, there should always be *something* clicking at any given time.

Writing things down and making lists puts my mind at ease because it gives me the sense that I am already on my way to getting things under control when I go to bed. Then in the morning, my lists give me a head start, a jump on the day. When I get up on Monday, usually around four A.M., I'll go to the gym to work out, then when I go home, after cleaning up, I'll get to work on the things on my list for the week.

I've got a list of things that I want to have done before I even leave the house. I'll make breakfast for my kids and spend a little time with them, which is probably the most important job of the day. I'll make some phone calls to people in the eastern time zones who are already well into their workday, and then, by the time I head for the office, I'm rocking and rolling.

Having a daily plan of attack is only one small step toward getting on course, but it does give you a feel for the value of having a plan. Try it for tomorrow. Make a list of at least three things you can do to move you closer to your Ultimate Goal, whatever that may be. Now, remember, your Ultimate Goal shouldn't be some material thing like: "to own a Ferrari Testarossa." It should relate more generally to the direction you want your life to take, one that is compatible with your talents, interests, and values.

What can you do tomorrow to go after your Ultimate Goal? I advise you to set smaller goals that will move you closer to the Ultimate Goal. Get a piece of paper now and at the top of it write your Ultimate Goal. Then, write things that you can do, steps you can take, to move you toward it tomorrow, next week, next month, next year, within five years, and within ten years.

Now take that piece of paper, hold it up, and look at it. Congratulations! You have *a plan*. Feels great, doesn't it? Do you know why? Because now you have the basic outline of the script for PowerLiving. You have taken the controls. You aren't waiting for life to happen to you anymore. You have a plan to make things happen. Believe me, once you get a plan and start following it, from tomorrow to next week and beyond, your life will change dramatically.

Getting into the Flow of Life

Psychologists have long wondered why it is that some people love their work, have wonderful relationships with their families and friends, and enjoy life enormously, while other people claim to hate their jobs, feel bored at both work and home, and in general find life to be a drag.

A psychologist at the University of Chicago, Mihaly Csikzent-mihalyi, developed the concept of flow after studying creativity. He found that highly creative people generally seemed to be happier and more balanced individuals than noncreative people. He wondered how more people might be able to transform their humdrum lives into meaningful, exciting, and happy ones.

After years of researching why certain people seem to take such joy in their lives while others do not, he found that a lot of people who seemed to enjoy their lives talked about being "in the flow." That is how they described the feeling they get when they were so involved in their work or their favorite activity that they forgot about everything else around them—time, their challenges, and other distractions that tend to drive people batty.

What surprised the psychologist and his researchers was that this sense of being in the flow occurred not while people were watching reruns of *Gilligan's Island* or otherwise relaxing or entertaining themselves, but rather when they were working at something that challenged them and stretched them physically or mentally.

It seems that people get more of a sense of flow from working on jobs that they enjoy than from leisure activities. The psychologists discovered that when people are involved in something that demands the use of their talents and abilities at the highest levels, they enter "a rare state of consciousness." The first symptom of this is "a narrowing of attention on a clearly defined goal," the researchers reported.

I'm not Sigmund Freud (or even Siegfried and Roy), but I understand what these researchers are talking about because I've been in the flow for quite a while now. I enjoy the heck out of my businesses, my family, and my life in general because I am always working on a plan that is part of PowerLiving. I fit the researchers' profile of someone who is living in the flow. Yes, I'm one of the Fabulous Flow People. Peace, happiness, and planning.

Seriously, Csikzentmihalyi found that when people get involved in, focused on, and absorbed in what they are doing—when they are following a specific plan for their lives—then they feel better about themselves and everything they do. You often hear about athletes—of all types, from professional quarterbacks and basketball players to women skiers or tennis players—being in the flow. Martina Navratilova won nine Wimbledon women's singles championships between 1978 and 1990—more than any other player—because she was a master of getting into the flow of her sport.

Basketball, like tennis, is a sport in which athletes often talk about "being in the flow." In the 1997 All-Star Game, Glen Rice of the Charlotte Hornets won the Most Valuable Player award because he was so obviously in the flow. Rice scored twenty points in one quarter, to put the East ahead and set an All-Star Game record. Afterward, he talked about what it is like to be in the flow as an athlete. "Sometimes you see the basketball going in before you release it, you feel everything you throw up is going in and it's one of the greatest feelings you can imagine."

I'll bet that you have been in the flow many times without realizing it. Have you ever been working on a project when you suddenly realized that you had no idea where the time went or that the stereo was on but you had no idea what it was playing? Chances are, you were in the flow. Usually it occurs when you are totally engrossed in something that you enjoy because you are good at it or because it is important to you. I often get into the flow when I am working out every morning. I also use that time to think about my goals for the day. More and more, I find that I get in the flow while conducting business. If I have a major deal to put together, I am at the point now in my career where I know whom I have to call and what I have to do to make a deal work.

The University of Chicago researchers found that accomplished musicians, computer programmers, and surgeons frequently report a sense of flow. But the psychologists also found that everyday activities or jobs can also become exciting and involving, "once the challenges are brought into balance with the person's skills and the goals." When you have goals and a plan, you prepare yourself to get into the flow. When you use your skills and talents to follow a plan of attack to achieve your Ultimate Goal, you gain a sense of control over your life.

The researchers who studied the phenomenon of flow say it comes as close as anything they have found to what most people describe as "happiness." From their studies, they feel that to be truly happy, you have to be involved in something that meets these four criteria.

1. It must involve concrete goals and manageable rules.
2. It must provide opportunities that are within your abilities to act.
3. It must give you regular feedback on how well you are doing.
4. It must screen out distractions and make concentration possible.

What activity meets all of those criteria? *Working on a plan.* When you create a plan to go after your Ultimate Goal,

1. You give structure to your life by setting manageable goals and concrete rules for going after them.
2. You prepare yourself to take advantage of every opportunity and to make the most of even those opportunities that might first appear to be limited.
3. You always know where you are and how you are doing in relation to your Ultimate Goal.
4. You become focused so that distractions and challenges don't throw you off course.

I've got a wacky example of this for you. Back when I was still trying to break into acting, my agent sent me to an audition for a television series based on the movie *The Four Seasons,* which Alan Alda had written, directed, and starred in. I had no idea what the part was, but I trusted my agent, who said they were looking for "all-American" types. When I walked into the waiting room for the casting call, though, I lost all trust in my agent's judgment.

The waiting room was packed with what looked like a Hell's Angels convention. My first thought was "What the heck am I doing here?" My second thought was "I am going to kill my agent."

I was sorely tempted to turn around and walk out of there, but even though this looked like an extremely limited opportunity, I decided to go for it. If it was part of my plan to expand my brand as an actor, then I had to at least see what this role was and give it my best shot. And so I waited along with the Harley boys until the receptionist called my name.

She led me into the interview room, where the casting director handed me a script and asked me to read for the part of the leader of the pack, the Head Biker. I read it with an all-American smile, not a snarl, and to my surprise they bought it.

"Very good, Mr. Steinfeld. Could you do the part riding a motorcycle?"

"Absolutely," I lied.

I had never been on a motorcycle in my life.

But they didn't know that. The casting director told me they would be in touch. I went home and immediately put in a phone call to my agent, prepared to give her an earful about sending me to a casting call for bikers. But before I could say anything, she said, "Congratulations, you got the part. They tape in two days and they want you to ride a motorcycle."

What motorcycle?

"You do ride a motorcycle, don't you?"

"No."

"Well, I suggest that sometime between now and Thursday you learn, if you want the part," she said.

What can I say? It was part of the plan. I had to go for it. I called a buddy who is a movie stuntman and he agreed to get a motorcycle and to meet me in the parking lot of a grade-school playground in Studio City. The motorcycle he brought was a little Honda 250, which weighed about as much as the saddlebags on a Harley chopper. It was a good thing. I had a hard enough time mastering the mechanics of the baby bike.

My buddy spent about six hours teaching me the basics of motorcycle riding. He set up cones, and kept putting them back up after I'd plow them over. Finally he said I was ready for the road. "As long as you aren't playing Evel Knievel, you should be able to handle it," my buddy said.

I reported to the set the next day, where twenty serious bikers waited for me, their leader. They all had customized Harleys that looked like they'd come out of the Road Warrior's garage. The director called me over and said, "Jake, you can ride this one for your scene."

He pointed to one of the biggest and wildest-looking Harleys, which, by coincidence, was being ridden by one of the biggest and wildest-looking guys. It immediately occurred to me that if I put so much as a smudge on his motorcycle, I probably could say good-bye to at least five or six teeth. This guy was wearing a fifty-pound chain as a necklace.

I walked over to the gentleman, and in a quiet voice that the director could not hear I said, "You don't want me to ride your hawg."

"Naw, it's okay, Jake, you'll do fine. You've ridden before, right?"

At this point, every member of the Wild Bunch was staring at me. To make matters worse, the director brought over my designated "biker chick." "She'll ride with you," he said.

Great. Not only was I going to crash this monster's motorcycle, angering him and ruining my acting career before it even got kick-started, but I was probably going to endanger the life of this leather-bound babe, too.

"Do me a favor. Tell the director I smell and you don't want to get near me. I don't want to kill you along with myself," I whispered to her.

She looked at me as if I had inhaled too much exhaust. Then she climbed on behind me. I couldn't hide it anymore. When I nearly drove through the camera crew on the first take, it became obvious that I had no idea how to ride the Harley. But the director didn't want to waste time finding another Head Biker, so he finessed the scene.

If you ever see the episode, you will be treated to a vision of Big Jake riding into view with my biker babe on the back of the Harley, but you may notice that you never see the whole rear end of the bike. That's because there were three or four guys *pushing* us into the camera's view. I look like a real cool dude with my legs up high on the motorcycle and my hair blowing in the wind, thanks to a high-powered fan and the magic of Hollywood.

But hey, *it was all part of the plan, man.*

When you go with the flow and follow a plan, opportunities appear and things seem to work out. Having a plan puts you in the flow of life and makes you happier than you have ever been before. It's true. Believe me, as a guy who once was without a plan, I know. When I was enrolled in college without knowing what I really wanted to do, and feeling like I really didn't belong there, I was seriously *out* of the flow. Even though I had some good times and made some good friends in my short college career, I wasn't really happy. My life didn't meet any of the four criteria for happiness listed above. I didn't have any concrete goals. I was totally unprepared for opportunity because I wouldn't have recognized it if it had hit me over the head. I had no idea what I was doing. And an invitation to go sledding on a cafeteria tray was enough to distract me for hours because I wasn't committed to college. In general, I just didn't feel good about myself.

In their study of flow, the Chicago psychologists found that self-esteem is generally not a constant, that it fluctuates during each day according to the environment and each person's individual performance. When you are in the flow, you tend to feel satisfied with your performance and you also feel good about how you are doing and feel good that you are living up to your own expectations as well as those of people whose judgment you value. The researchers found that people who regularly experience flow are more likely to have higher overall levels of self-esteem than people who don't.

A Family Plan

My younger sister Nancy discovered the value of having a plan just recently while searching for a new job. For a while there, Nancy was just content to let life happen to her. She wasn't doing badly. She had a good job in the advertising department of one of the studios in Hollywood, but she wasn't happy because it wasn't really what she wanted to be doing. She didn't think it was the best use of her talents, interests, and intelligence. In other words, she wanted to get in the flow. Her real dream was to get into marketing and promotions with a big studio. She had a choice of two offers and actually took the one that paid less but was more in line with her goals. Now she is in a good position to reach her Ultimate Goal. She is back in the flow.

When you are creating your plan, keep in mind that the best way to get into the flow is to allocate your time, energy, and resources wisely. What you are really doing when you devise a plan is making the decision to take control of your life by plotting a course detailing what you do each day, week, month, and year. You are consciously standing up and saying, "I'm in charge. Nobody else is going to tell me what to do. Nothing is going to throw me off."

The steps you take each day reflect your determination and priorities in going after your Ultimate Goal. The decisions and actions you take each day determine whether or not you will reach your goals. One of the most important decisions you will make when creating your plan is to assess what is truly important and what is within your control, so that you can decide what to focus on to achieve your Ultimate Goal.

Making the Right Choices

As I watch my kids grow, I see them gradually come to understand that there are things they can control, like me and the VCR, and things that are out of their control, like the cat, which always has its own plan. As adults, people sometimes forget the difference. A lot of people waste time trying to control things that are beyond their reach. For example, it really does no good to worry about what other people say about you, because you can't control that unless you are the dictator of some Third World country and have a lot of free prison space. On the other hand, you can control how you choose to respond to criticism or unkind words from other

people. You don't have to let their words or actions have a negative impact on you.

The important thing to remember is that you have only so much
time on this earth to go after your Ultimate Goal, so it's wise to
concentrate only on those things that you can control and to focus
on taking those actions that are most important in achieving your
goals.

The biggest obstacle you may encounter when you try to follow
your plan is the distraction of things that demand to be done immediately. These are things that don't really have anything to do
with your Ultimate Goal, but they distract you from attending to
the things that are really important to your goal.

What sort of demanding but unimportant things am I talking
about? There are all kinds of demanding but unimportant things
that can throw you off course. Say your master plan has a critical
step that involves enrolling in college to get a more advanced degree. Tuition will set you back a couple thousand dollars. You
have the money, but you also feel you need to buy a new car. Your
old car is still working, but it is a wreck. If you spend the money
to resolve the demanding but less critical need for a newer car,
rather than using the money to pay your college tuition, you have
been knocked off course.

Right now, get a piece of paper and make a list of the things that
are truly *vital* to your plan for your life, and next to that column
make a list of the things that are simply demanding but not vital.
Make up your mind that you are going to stay focused only on
those things that move you most quickly toward your goals.

Many Paths to Your Destination

While it is vital to have a goal and a plan, it is equally important to
understand that there may be many different routes to your destination. Of all the people I know who are successful actors or entertainment industry executives, I don't know any two of them who
followed exactly the same path to reach their position. Even executives who hold the same jobs at different studios followed widely

divergent paths to get there. Take the hint. Understand just as the ship's captain does when he leaves the port of departure that unforeseen factors like weather, wind, or mass mutiny may force him to alter his course en route to his destination.

It would be great if we could all sit down at the age of seventeen or eighteen and say, This is my Ultimate Goal, and this is the straight road I am going to take to get there. But you can't say, I am going to do this, and then this, and then this, and in twenty years I will be exactly where I want to be. The reality is that your path will take many unexpected turns. That is part of the fun of the journey.

The important thing is to be headed in the right direction and always moving toward your Ultimate Goal, rather than being stuck, or moving in the opposite direction. When you have a plan in place, it moves you step by step toward your goals. It puts you in the flow of life. And that is *exactly* what PowerLiving is!

POWERLIVING
LESSON NO. 5

Find Yourself a Myra Duberstein

At the beginning of this book I told you that I wasn't *really* going to be telling you stories about seeing famous people naked. Remember? Well, I lied. I do have one story to share with you that would not betray any confidences or bring the legal sharks to my office door. There is one star that I saw naked, although at the time, he was just one more . . . ahh . . . face in the crowd. It was the actor Keith Carradine.

I met Keith in person, and with his clothes on, when I was training my very first client, Sandy Will, who just happened to be his girlfriend (and future wife). I started training Keith too, and one day after a workout, he mentioned that he had performed in one of the original casts of the rock musical *Hair.*

I told him that I had seen *Hair* on Broadway when I was just a kid. When I told him the year I'd seen it, Keith started laughing.

What's so funny?

"Jake, I can't believe it. You've seen me naked!" he said.

He was right. In one of the scenes of the musical, the entire cast came out from under a big sheet, naked. I hope I didn't hurt his feelings, but I didn't recall Keith standing out in the crowd. The funniest aspect of that story is that it was my grandma who took me to see the musical, though I think she put her scarf over my eyes during the nude scene.

Yes, my escort to *Hair* was my grandma, the inimitable, the irrepressible, the absolutely incredible Myra Duberstein. Until her death, when I was twenty years old, Grams was my biggest champion. More than anybody else, she believed that I was destined to be somebody. More important, she made me believe it too. Her faith in me helped me through some challenging times in my life, and she did everything she could to expand my view of the possibilities awaiting me in the world. To this day, in fact, I keep her gold necklace with her initials on it on top of my desk. She meant so much to me and she believed that so much was possible for me, I keep the necklace as a reminder that I don't ever want to let her down. Instead, I want to build on what she gave me, and whenever possible, I want to be as supportive of the people I care about as my grandma was of me.

Get a Go-To Person

So far, I've shown you how to strive for self-awareness so that you can become the person you need to become to get where you want to go in life. I have also helped you learn how to set goals for your life by using your imagination to dream big, and I have shown you how to act on those big dreams by coming up with a plan. In this chapter, I want to help you select what I call a Go-To Person to help you go after your Ultimate Goal.

What is a Go-To Person? In sports, I guess you'd have to say one of the best known is Michael Jordan. He is the guy on the NBA World Championship team that everybody *goes to* when they need a clutch basket or a big play. Scottie Pippen and Toni Kukoc and the other Bulls are all very good players, but Michael is the guy they all know they can rely on most of the time to be there and to lift them all up. That's the mark of a real Go-To Person. Your Go-To Person is the person in your life who is always there for you, who believes in you and your dreams, and is willing to help you in any way possible.

When you go after your Ultimate Goal, it will not always be easy. There will be challenging times. Not everyone will share your dream and your vision for your life. Some may even try to hold you back or block your path, out of jealousy, self-interest, or other reasons. That is why I believe everyone needs a Go-To Person. Certainly you have to take responsibility for your own life. Ultimately, your success is up to you and no one else. That doesn't mean you are expected to go it alone. We all need backup support from time to time. We all need someone willing to cheer us on and to keep us on target, a positive source that we can go to when our own batteries are running low.

The *last* thing you need when you are faced with a challenge or a setback is someone who offers negative reinforcement or, worse yet, someone who says, "I told you so." Sooner or later in your life or career, you will find yourself in an environment that is absolutely poisoned with negativity by people who are out of the flow and unhappy with their lives. There is only one way to deal with this situation. Do not try to change them. That is not your responsibility, and chances are you couldn't accomplish it in your lifetime. No, my best advice in this situation is very simple: *Run!* These are not Go-To People; these are Run-From People.

Get out of their grasp as fast and as gracefully as you can. If it is your office environment that is leaking poisonous negativity, get a transfer or find another place to work. You cannot afford to be weighed down by the disappointments and bitterness and bad attitudes of other people. You don't have to be the office Pollyanna, but negative people can kill your career.

Poisonous people get their fangs in you and kill your dreams if you allow them to get inside your head. It may seem cool at first to be cynical and sarcastic, but that attitude will only weigh you down. Often, the company you keep can have a huge impact on your ability to pursue your dreams and goals.

Take a time out here and reflect on those around you and their impact on your life. Do your friends make you better or do they drag you down? Do they have high expectations of you or could they care less about your growth and development? Are their own lives on an upward spiral, or are they stuck or, worse, in a tailspin? Whom can you go to when you need a boost? Do you have positive friends who are on the rise and eager to see you rise with them? If you don't, isn't it time you went out and built those kinds of mutually supportive relationships?

An Investment That Pays for Years

My Grams really made a huge investment of time, and probably money, too, in trying to prepare me for success. It's funny. I used to think she was rich and famous because my grandma seemed to know everybody in New York City. The truth is, she was wealthy only in spirit. She managed the Manhattan Beach Hotel in New York, where a lot of famous people passed through. She befriended them all. The singers Neil Sedaka and Neil Diamond were both bar mitzvahed at the Manhattan Beach. Former New York Knicks star Walt Frazier conducted a seminar there once and my grandma got me into it. I loved hanging around her hotel, working the coat check and making tips. My grandma wanted me to see more of the world than Brooklyn, and she took it upon herself to be my guide.

Through her hotel contacts, she was able to get tickets and great seats to seemingly any event in the city of New York. She took me to tennis matches at Forest Hills, to Mets games, to the horse races at Aqueduct and Belmont Raceway, to ski resorts in upstate New York, to the fights, to plays, concerts, movies—you name it, she had a ticket for it. Or at least she knew the guy guarding the back entrance. For my sixth birthday, she took me to Madison Square Garden to see the fights, and somehow she got the great fighter Jack Dempsey to pose with me on his lap. I still have that photograph.

She didn't just escort me; she made sure that I saw all there was to see. If she spied a movie star or a star athlete in the crowd, she marched me up to whoever it was and introduced both herself and me as if we too were celebrities. I probably have childhood photos of myself with more Hollywood stars and sports heroes than any other kid from Long Island. More autographs, too. I'll never forget when I was eight years old, she took me right up to the Mets dugout after the game and asked Tom Seaver and the catcher Jerry Grote to sign my baseball glove. Seaver signed it, but Grote ignored us. My Go-To Grandma gave him a piece of her mind and then turned to me and said, "When you're famous, don't ever be like that man."

I looked at her in disbelief. Me, famous? What are you talking about? It was just her way of letting me know she believed in me, and when you have someone who believes that strongly in your potential, you begin to believe that it really may be true, that there really may be something special out there waiting for you.

Larger Than Life

One of the last bodybuilding competitions I entered was also the last one my grandma was able to attend. It was the Mr. Southern California contest in Los Angeles, and she flew out to see me, even though she was not feeling well. Her health was deteriorating badly, but she wanted to be there for me and I wanted to win for her. But I came in second.

"Don't worry about it; you will win the next one," she told me.

My grandma died six weeks later, but her spirit is with me. I hear her voice encouraging me every time I face a challenge, and I thank her every time I overcome one and reach a goal.

Hers was the first funeral I ever attended. At Jewish funerals, the coffin is kept closed, but afterward friends and family sit *shiva*, which involves, among other things, telling stories about the person who died. During the service for her, I wandered around the room thinking about all she had done for me. Suddenly, I found myself standing next to her casket, and my knees began to shake. I was twenty years old and I felt that I had lost the most important person in my life. My champion. My Go-To Person. My inspiration.

When I looked at the coffin, I was struck by how small it seemed. My grandma was only five feet, four inches tall, but she had always seemed so much bigger than that to me. She was such a major presence in my life. She was bigger than life to me. She taught me the value of building and maintaining mutually supportive relationships. And most of all, she taught me never to quit. She defined PowerLiving!

When you have doubts or face serious challenges on the way to your Ultimate Goal, it can be of enormous help to have someone there standing beside you ready to say, "I know you can do it. I've got faith in you. You are on the right track. Go for it." Not that your Go-To Person has to be a yes-person. You don't want someone who isn't willing to tell you that maybe you are headed in the wrong direction. You do want someone who is always looking out for your best interests, even when you may not be able to see the way yourself.

Your Go-To Person Pumps You Up

When I was eighteen years old and very much into weight training, I was desperate to go see a new movie documentary about competitive bodybuilding called *Pumping Iron.* My grandma somehow got tickets to a special preview in Manhattan. I couldn't believe it. Grams was like a guardian angel who always seemed to come to the rescue. She had always encouraged me to read and get an education, but she also was willing to support me in my dream of bodybuilding.

Pumping Iron starred a guy I really admired back then—a guy who is a neighbor of mine today—Arnold Schwarzenegger. He wasn't a big movie star or major celebrity yet, except in the bodybuilding world, where he was more or less a god. Arnold was the featured guy in *Pumping Iron,* which helped launch his film career. I was in awe of him, and my big hope was that he would be at the premiere. Grams knew how I felt, so when we got to the theater, which was packed with well-dressed people, she helped me scout around for him. We didn't see him and I was more than a little bummed out. After the movie, she and I got out quickly so we could look for Arnold again. She spied him first, standing in the theater lobby all by himself, waiting for the rest of the people to come out. Grams pointed him out and I walked over to him and shook his hand . . . and kept shaking it.

I was seriously tongue-tied. I stood there unable to speak. I'd been into bodybuilding for about four years at that point, and I ate, slept, and drank it. I had all the muscle magazines, and Arnold was on the cover of most of them. For me, this was like an audience with the pope. I was dumbstruck. I can't remember if I ever said anything. All I know is that when I started shaking his hand the theater lobby was empty, and by the time Arnold got his hand back, it was packed. Before I could say anything coherent, Arnold had been swept away by the departing crowd.

My grandma couldn't believe that I had been too stunned to utter a word. "Do you want to talk to him or not?" she asked. When I nodded in the affirmative, she grabbed my hand and led me back through the crowd, which was rapidly thinning out. In the distance we could see the massive figure of Arnold and his girlfriend walking down Fifth Avenue. Towing me like a tugboat with a big dinghy behind it, Grams chased Arnold until we got within shouting distance. "Excuse me, Mr. Schwarz-EN-egger, my grandson here would like to talk with you," she announced.

Arnold stopped and waited. The future Terminator realized that not even he could shake Myra Duberstein when she was on a mission for her grandson. I'll give him credit: He was patient with his fans even then. "Did you like the movie?" Arnold asked us.

Again, nothing. Lip lock set in.

"Jake, do you have a question for Mr. Schwarzenegger?" my grandma said in exasperation.

The best I could come up with was "Wha-wha-what do you do to build up your calf muscles?"

I don't even remember what Arnold's response was. I do recall that it seemed like the world was suddenly in slow motion as he said something, and then shook my hand again, smiled at me and Grams, and then quickly disappeared into the night. I do recall the look Grams gave me. For a brief second, I thought she was going to belt her favorite grandson with her purse.

Your Go-To Greases the Way

That's another good thing about having a Go-To Person. A Go-To Person is not only on your side, but she can also set you straight when you seem to be drifting out of control or losing sight of your Ultimate Goal. Just as every writer needs an editor and every ath-

lete needs a coach, every person chasing after a dream needs someone not only to support and encourage him but also to push and
occasionally to whip him into line. You may think you are perfectly
capable of keeping yourself focused on your goals, and maybe you
are. But it doesn't hurt to have someone there to belt you with a
purse, or somehow to let you know that you aren't paying enough
attention. You know that your Go-To Person is seriously behind
you when she takes that kind of interest in your success.

You can't expect everybody to step up. Before I entered my first
competition, I was trying to find someone to teach me how to pose.
At the gym where I trained, a place called FutureMan in Amityville,
Long Island, the manager was a guy who had won the Mr. Apollo
contest. He was the first real bodybuilder I'd ever met. I walked up
to him in the gym one day and told him I was going to enter my
first contest. I asked if he would help me with a posing routine. He
looked at me and said, "No." I was stunned. Later, the assistant
manager said, "He won't help you because he thinks you would be
competition for him. Your shoulders are already bigger than his."

Have you ever heard the saying "Nobody wants to see their
friends succeed"? That's a cynical view of friendship, and I don't
think it holds for true friends. There is always competition among
friends, but the people who really care about you want to see you
succeed. They buy in to your dreams and goals. My grandma
adopted my dream of bodybuilding as if it were her own. If she
could have worked out with me every morning, she would have
been right there pumping iron with me. If she could have helped
me lift the weights, she would have done it. She did accompany me
to some of my first competitions and she even helped cover me
with tanning oil so my muscles would look good under the lights.
I remember her helping my brother Peter put Sudden Tan on me in
preparation for my first competition; it was for the region of
Delaware, Maryland, and Virginia so it was called the Mr. Del-
marva Contest.

I had no idea how to pose for the judges. My plan was to just
watch the guys who went on stage before me and do whatever they
did. There were about thirty-five people in the competition and we
had to draw numbers out of a hat to determine the order that we
went on.

Guess who got number one? Yep, the rookie. I flashed back to photographs of competitions I had seen in magazines and then I went up on the stage and tried to do the moves. My grandma and brother had done such a good job of oiling me up that on my first pose, my hands slipped right off my hips. Amazingly, I was awarded fifth place; they gave me a plaque about the size of a slice of bread, but I was ecstatic. "I'm going to be Mr. America," I told my grandma.

"You're already Mr. America," she replied.

That's the way it always was with her. Grams was my very first Go-To Person, and I have been reaping the benefits of her love and guidance all of my life. I said she was my first Go-To Person because I have had several in my life, and I expect I may have a few more. (I do have a few good years left, you know.) It is like that for most people. If you think of life as a long journey, then you can think of your Go-To People as guides who take you a certain amount of the way, and then hand you off to the next guide. My grandma got me to the age of twenty, and then she passed me on to a succession of Go-To People who have helped me move up the mountain higher than I ever could have made it on my own.

My Go-To People have included professional bodybuilders who were more experienced than I and entertainment business geniuses like Steven Spielberg, who has helped me make the right choices in what is an extremely competitive and occasionally treacherous business. Believe me, I count myself extremely lucky to have the supportive friends I have in Hollywood. A few years after I got to know Wiels, I was offered a role as a costar in a new crime-fighter television series. My costar was to be a guy who had just come off a successful run with a similar show. He was a good guy, and a big guy, too. He was a character actor who mostly played himself in a cartoonish way that young kids really liked.

We met with a production company and a syndicator and it was an interesting proposition for me. It would definitely have increased my brand awareness and the money was very good, but there was something about the deal that wasn't sitting right with me. I went to one of my Go-To Guys: Wiels.

He didn't mince words.

"Stop!" he said just as I started to tell him about the proposed show and my role.

"I've got nothing against your costar, he's a nice guy, but do you really want to play second banana to a second banana?" he asked. "Forget about the television exposure for a minute and think about the business you are trying to build. How would this impact your brand as a serious businessman?"

Wiels was right, of course. He saw that I was headed down the wrong path if one of my goals was to establish my brand as a businessman. Playing a cartoonish character would have been a serious mistake. Back when nobody knew who I was, and before I had established brand recognition as a businessman, I had no problems taking on whatever was offered. In fact, in the really early days I played a crazed killer in a horror film called *Home Sweet Home*. I murdered an entire family during their Thanksgiving Day dinner! During the filming, if I caught a glimpse of myself in the car mirror on the way home at night, I'd scare myself. It took me weeks to get all the blood—cherry syrup—out of my clothes.

I could no longer afford to do that sort of stuff if I wanted bankers and consumers to take me seriously. If I had taken the crime-fighting television series and it had done well, I might have had some fun and made some decent money for a few years, but then I probably would have been typecast forever, and my options would have been limited.

Wiels came through with some solid advice for me. I only hope I can return the favor someday. That is an important point. This is a two-way street. You can't expect other people to be there for you all the time unless you are willing to step up for them. I have served as the Go-To Person for a whole bunch of friends. Understand that it takes time to develop a network of Go-To People. The relationship has to be built on mutual trust. If people sense that your only motivation for establishing a relationship is pure self-interest, you will never be able to build trust. You have to be willing to lend a hand if you expect others to do it for you. When you earn a reputation for being a stand-up Go-To Person, it is amazing the connections you can make.

Another Hollywood director who has been a good friend over the years is John Landis, the Chicago guy who worked his way up from bit player in *Battle for the Planet of the Apes* to production assistant, actor, and director of movies like *The Blues Brothers, An American Werewolf in London,* and *Coming to America.* John put me in a 1985 picture called *Into the Night*—I'm sure you remember it well. Actually, it was the first movie for me, and it featured a couple of other folks you might have heard of, Michelle Pfeiffer and Jeff Goldblum.

I've been friends with John ever since then, so I reached out to him a while back when two people I know were looking for writing work. They had worked with me on the situation comedy I created and starred in for the Family Channel. It was called *Big Brother Jake.* I liked their work, and so when we closed the series after one hundred well-received shows, I called John to see if he could help them; now they are part of his writing team and are doing very well. It's really gratifying to be able to serve as the Go-To Guy, particularly after so many people reached out for me in my early days.

My business as a fitness motivator was basically built on one person reaching out to another and recommending me. Sandy Will, Keith Carradine's girlfriend, put me in touch with a terrific actress named Colleen Camp, who sent me to John Landis, who introduced me to the producer Sean Daniel, who sent me over to Harrison Ford, which led to my work with Wiels, and then on to George Lucas, Morgan Fairchild, Priscilla Presley, Terri Garr, Bette Midler, and Sally Kellerman, one after another. That's the way the game is played, and if you can build a Go-To network like that, believe me, there will always be someone willing to stand up for you.

Everybody Needs Somebody Sometime

My Go-To network includes a wide range of people today. Of course, my wife, Tracey, has been an enormous source of help and support for me. She is always there for me and she knows me better than I know myself. Tracey also has a good perspective on the businesses. She helps by standing back and looking at the big picture. Sometimes it's tough to hear from your wife that you are wrong, but if she can't say it to you, who can? She also has no qualms about correcting me in other areas of my life, such as my eating etiquette. It was Tracey who taught me that there is a difference between a buffet and a feeding trough. I can't help it, I get excited around food.

Looking for a Go-To

Who could serve as your primary Go-To Person? You may already have one among your friends and relatives. Is there someone who always seems to take an interest in you? Is there someone who appears to be on your side? An uncle, aunt, cousin, older brother or sister? My son Nicky's Go-To Person right now isn't a person at all. It's his blanket. When he is upset, he goes to his blanket and wraps it around himself. It comforts him and makes him feel secure.

Since you are probably a little beyond the age where you can be seen in public with your blankie, how do you attract or identify Go-To People? That is an important question. Here are important tips.

1. *You have to be fully committed and passionate about your dream.*

   The best way to attract Go-To People who will help you is to exhibit a passion and commitment for whatever it is you seek to do. When more experienced people see someone who is excited and committed, they are drawn to them. They reach out. Look at it from their point of view. Whom would you be more inclined to help, someone who was putting out every effort to succeed but still struggling, or someone who was making no effort to help herself or himself?

   If you are going to inspire other people to buy in to your dreams, you first have to exhibit that you have fully invested your own energies and talents in them.

2. *Look for people who are where you want to be, go to them, and ask for their advice and help.*

As I noted earlier, when I was doing the *Big Brother Jake* sitcom on the Family Channel, I became friends with Tim Robertson, who was the channel's cofounder and who serves as its president and CEO. Tim is a first-class individual, the sort of guy you quickly learn to trust and confide in. I told him my dreams of creating a cable television network devoted to fitness and health, and he immediately bought in to my dream. Tim guided me through the process of creating FiT TV. He gave me the benefit of his experiences with the creation of the Family Channel. It was like getting four years of college and a master's degree, too, all in conversations with a friend who believed in what I was doing.

3. *Find someone going in the same direction as you and become a tag team.*

When I was doing the *Fitness Break by Jake* on CNN, there was a guy at Turner Broadcasting, Rich Mel, who is about the same age as me, and we more or less adopted each other as partners in our climb up the ladder, even though we were on two entirely different career paths. We have stayed in touch over the years. He is now a highly respected multi-media entrepreneur. We probably talk once a week, comparing notes on everything from our work to parenthood.

It's nice to have this sort of person to go to just as a reference point. We don't make demands on each other, although I am sure he could count on me and I could count on him.

Parental Protection

When you are younger, often your Go-To Person might be a parent, or both parents. You are lucky if you have parents who can put their own wishes and desires for you aside and give you their full support when you go after what *you* want. But often that can be extremely difficult for parents to do. They have so much invested in you emotionally that they often are afraid to see you do something risky or out of the ordinary. It's not that they don't wish you well, but often parents can't bear to see you learn by trial and error. In other cases, your parents may not understand your dream, or out of their love for you and their desire to see things go smoothly, they may encourage you to select goals different from those that truly reflect *your* dreams. They may want the wrong things for you for legitimate reasons. They have a lot of love and time invested in you and they feel responsible not only for your happiness but also for your safety and security.

My parents were supportive of me, but they had their own dreams for me. I understand that, particularly now that I am a parent myself. While they encouraged me to take an interest in fitness and they could see how much I benefited from it, my parents were not enthusiastic at all about my dreams of becoming a competitive bodybuilder. It just was not something that fit their image of what a nice boy from Long Island should aspire to. *A doctor, a dentist, a lawyer, yes. Mr. America? How is that going to put bread on the table?*

Of course, my parents weren't alone in their disappointment at my career choice. After I had moved to Los Angeles, one of the first jobs I fell into was playing the Incredible Hulk for tourists at the Universal Studios Tour. I was offered the job because my body and my facial structure resembled that of Lou Ferrigno, who played the role of the angst-ridden green muscle man on the television series. This was no cakewalk job. I had to be the Hulk twelve times a day, wearing a fake nose, a green yak-hair wig, and green water-based paint in 95-degree heat, which meant I had to be repainted about twelve times a day, too. It wasn't exactly art of the highest form, but it was my first step into show business. Not everybody saw it that way, however. At the end of the performance, the show's host would introduce all of the players. One day, an elderly Jewish couple came through on the tour, and when they heard that the Hulk was played by Mr. Jake Steinfeld, they came up to me while I was signing autographs. Standing there in their Bermuda shorts and high white socks, they eyeballed me critically for a while before they worked up the courage to speak out: "Steinfeld?"

"Yes, sir. Do you folks know my parents?" I asked.

"Steinfeld? You're a Jewish boy? Doesn't that hurt when you make those muscles?"

I thought they were kidding, and I kept asking them if they knew my parents or something. "We wish we did know your parents. If we did, we would give them a piece of our minds about a Jewish boy doing this kind of work."

Like my parents, these folks wanted me to play by the rules of their generation. My grandma understood that each of us has to find his own way, and sometimes the hard way can be the right way. She encouraged me when I wanted to play by my own rules. She may secretly have agreed with my parents, but she never let me know. Grams understood that what I needed was the gentle guidance of a Go-To Person who, more than anything else, wanted to see me find my own way to my dreams and goals. Before you go on to the next chapter, get started on building your own Go-To network. And remember: *You gotta get a Go-To Person to get where you want to go!*

POWERLIVING
LESSON NO. 6

Build Your Brand

When I was just getting started with the Body by Jake licensing and marketing business, I was offered an extremely tempting deal by a brewing company that makes a nonalcoholic beer. They wanted me to be the spokesman for their product, sort of a human version of the Budweiser frogs. They wanted me to endorse their nonalcoholic beer as a healthier alternative to regular beer, and they offered me a substantial amount of money to do it.

I have nothing against anyone who endorses beer, near-beer, or even tap water, for that matter. If a bunch of frogs can get an agent and make a few bucks with Bud, I say, "Go for it, Kermit!" But I wasn't inclined to jump at this deal myself. If money had been my number one priority at that point—and believe me, it wasn't *real* far down the list—I probably would have made the leap because the deal would have taken care of most of my bills, and then some. As tempting as the offer was financially, I told them I would have to think about it.

Up to that point I had worked to develop an image as an advocate of healthy living, and I wasn't sure that even a nonalcoholic beer was something I wanted to be associated with. I just had this feeling in my gut that this sort of endorsement would put me in a position that might be difficult to explain or maneuver out of later.

If it had been an alcoholic beverage, a beer or liquor brand, the decision would have been a lot easier: I wouldn't have done it. But this was a grayer area, so I decided to seek the counsel of someone with deeper experience.

I didn't have to look far for good advice. Through Steven Spielberg, I'd been fortunate to meet one of the smartest businessmen in the entertainment industry, the late Steve Ross. A Hollywood legend, Steve had taken a string of funeral parlors in Brooklyn and built an empire of car rentals, parking lots, and cleaning services, which he then leveraged into ownership of Warner Bros. Studio. Eventually, he engineered the Time Warner merger.

Over the years, Steve had become Wiels's best friend and adviser. Wiels called him "the single most generous person I have ever met in my life"—Ross was probably the Go-To Guy for half of Hollywood. He did more favors for more people than anyone else in show business. I was just one of many whom he helped.

Given his business sense and his concern for others, I considered Steve an excellent source of advice, so when I had the chance I asked him what he thought of the offer from the nonalcoholic beer company. He responded with a serious lecture on the importance of protecting my brand in the marketplace. He told me to envision a life-size cutout picture of myself placed in the beer and alcohol section of a supermarket. Mothers would walk by with their kids in shopping carts. Teenagers would take punches at me. The exposure would be great, Steve said, but just over my shoulder would be cases of beer, and rows of wine, scotch, vodka, bourbon, and other alcohol products.

"Sure, you might be holding two six-packs of nonalcoholic beer in the cutout, but kids and their parents would focus on the image of Jake with beer," Steve told me. "Don't do it. It will hurt your brand recognition and you don't need that. Even though the money looks good, you have to think of protecting your brand over the long term."

Brand Recognition

I had never taken a marketing class, nor had I gone to business school, but Steve Ross was only reinforcing what I have always understood instinctively: You have to establish and then protect your brand as a *person* and as a *product* in the marketplace, no matter what sort of business you are involved in.

What is your brand? Well, like the brand on the hindquarters of a Texas longhorn, which tells the cowpokes where the steer comes from, your brand is your identity in the marketplace and in the world around you.

General Motors has its brands such as Chevrolet, Buick, and Cadillac, and each of those brands represents something unique. Chevrolet is primarily seen as a brand of practical and economical cars. Buick represents a bit more luxury, while Cadillac is seen as a top-of-the-line, prestige vehicle. You can bet that once General Motors and any other car company establishes the identity of each of its brands, it closely guards the integrity of each brand name so that the buyer knows what to expect from each of them. That only makes good business sense.

The same holds true for you, whether in business or in relationships. I've shown you so far that to get your life into a continuous upward spiral of achievement and fulfillment, you first have to use your imagination to determine what it is you want to do with your life and establish goals, including your Ultimate Goal. Then you must form a plan to get there and take small steps each day to stay on the path to your dreams and goals. But since life has a way of presenting all sorts of obstacles, challenges, and alternative routes, how will you know which way to go? In this chapter, I will teach you to establish your brand by selecting values and principles that will serve as guidelines and path markers. I will show you the importance of having a well-defined brand identity and I will also demonstrate the value of protecting the integrity of your brand by sticking with those values and principles.

If you haven't been getting what you want out of life, particularly in your job or career, it might be that part of the challenge is due to a lack of *brand recognition*. Have you ever thought about what you represent as a person, or as a product in the marketplace? When people think of you, do they think of someone they can depend on? Do they consider you a trustworthy person with high moral and ethical standards? Or does your brand represent something less?

I am not suggesting that your goal should be to live up to standards to please other people. I am advising you, though, that the way you live your life and the standards you set for *yourself* have a very big impact on the way other people perceive you. Why is it that most top banking executives dress conservatively? Because they have a brand image to protect. Would you rather place your financial health in the hands of someone who appears to be meticulous, well balanced, and dedicated to his work or with someone who wears a nose ring?

Do you see the importance now of creating a brand image for yourself? If you don't see it now, sooner or later it will hit you over the head. Pick up any business magazine these days and you'll see a lot of references to the explosion in entrepreneurship around the world. This is a global trend in employment. Fewer and fewer people will have long-term jobs with one company or business. Instead, more and more people will work as independent consultants or contract workers. In this environment, it will be absolutely vital to have an entrepreneurial mind-set in which *you* are the product. When the world is overrun with independent contractors and entrepreneurs, your brand image will be among your most important assets.

Thinking Like an Entrepreneur

With the crazed trend in downsizing, rightsizing, and mass beheadings in the last fifteen years, corporate America has thrown a lot of talented and well-educated people out onto the street. At first, this triggered a great deal of angst, but it has also helped set off an explosion in entrepreneurship across the country. What is an entrepreneur? It is someone who takes his or her talents, interests, and skills and creates a self-driven business. I am an entrepreneur, and so are millions of others. Dun & Bradstreet has been tracking the entrepreneur explosion by looking at the amazing growth of home-based business. They estimate that a new home-based business is launched every eleven seconds, that there are already more than 27 million full- and part-time home-based businesses in this country, and that by the start of 1998 there will be nearly 90 million home-based businesses in operation.

The wave of entrepreneurship has been set off in part by the fact that many companies that had downsized employees are now hiring them back, often as independent contractors or "outsourced" employees. Social scientists and others say that in the coming decades, the majority of people will be working in this manner, which will in effect make us a nation of entrepreneurs. More and more people will be living outside the corporate structure, and as a result, it will be up to all of us to motivate ourselves and guide our own careers. The new entrepreneurs may be involved in everything from catering meals to car detailing, from stock trading to pet grooming. No matter what your business or service may be, your brand image will set you apart from the competition.

Your brand is not just the name of your company or product; it is your reputation as a businessperson and also as an individual. Whether your dream is to be a successful businessperson or a successful artist, jet pilot, or parent, you should learn to think like an entrepreneur and to establish values and principles that protect your personal brand along the way.

As an entrepreneur, I've worked very carefully to build a brand that represents a healthy, family-oriented lifestyle. That is what I want people to associate with the Body by Jake brand and my image as a businessman and entertainer. I didn't want to compete for product endorsements or acting jobs with either Hulk Hogan or Arnold Schwarzenegger. They have their unique brands and their own markets and I know there is room for them and me— and Richard Simmons and Jane Fonda.

Enough Success to Go Around

When you believe that there is enough success to go around for everyone, that is what is known as having an "abundance mentality." Too often, people have a problem controlling their competitive instincts. They feel that in order to get ahead, they have to leave someone else behind, or that to climb to the top, they have to pull someone else down. That is known as a "scarcity mentality." It reflects a narrow view of life in which there is only so much success out there. For people who have this mentality, it's every man for himself. These individuals don't want to share anything—not success, not credit, not control, not rewards. They are generally not very happy people because when those around them succeed, they take it as a sign that they themselves are sliding backward. It doesn't have to be that way and you should not allow yourself to think that way, because while it may work for you in the short term, over the long haul it will only diminish your brand.

Adolf Hitler (this is called making a good example of a bad example) rose to leadership in Germany just as Winston Churchill came to be the leader of England. Yet history has entirely different perceptions of them. Hitler's leadership was built on a scarcity mentality. He rose to power by cultivating fear and hatred. He made scapegoats of the Jewish people and convinced his followers that the Jews had to be destroyed in order to clear the way for the success of his "master race." Churchill's power, on the other hand, was built on an abundance mentality. He cultivated greatness and pride. He told the people of England that the only thing they had to fear was "fear itself." He brought England through the war and the horrendous bombings by building the courage and moral strength of his country. When you base your brand value on an abundance mentality, you build a life and career rich in values, just as Winston Churchill did. People are drawn to you because they see that your life isn't about tearing down, it is about building up.

Building Your Brand

Okay, so how do you build *your* brand? By determining which values and principles will guide your life. In the marketplace of business and career, people want quality, consistency, and dependability from those they deal with, just as they do from the products or services they purchase. It is important that you establish a brand that meets those needs and expectations. I have worked to put my business and career on a high plane by dealing in high-quality products and family-oriented television programming. Because I have established that sort of brand identity, I have turned down all sorts of endorsement proposals, including one for a product called Fatty Clamps that supposedly let you watch the fat disappear as you worked out, sort of the "pinch-by-pinch, inch-by-inch method," if you get the picture.

We all face many choices and temptations as we pursue our dreams and goals. Your brand values and principles help you make the right decisions for yourself over the entire course of your lifetime. Do you remember when Oprah Winfrey found that her talk show's top ratings were being challenged by a small army of new talk-show hosts who took the format down the low road? For a year or so, talk shows took a dive into trash television. It became a contest of How Low Can You Go? For a time, the trash talk-show hosts challenged Oprah's preeminence in the ratings, but viewers quickly grew tired of the low road.

Although she was initially taken by surprise at the popularity of the trash TV hosts, Oprah quickly decided that she was not going to get into a mud-wrestling contest. Instead, she took her show to even higher levels. Instead of inviting demented and angry people on her show, she confounded the "experts" and began bringing on authors and discussing books. To the amazement of all, Oprah's ratings went higher than ever before. What made her so successful? She had faith in the strength of her brand as a television talk-show host and she stuck with it.

It is important to have strong brand values in your personal life also. If you are to have long-lasting and fulfilling relationships, people must see there is value for them in hooking up with you. They must feel that you are trustworthy and reliable and as concerned about their welfare as you are about your own. Can those around you rely on you? Are you innovative, self-motivated, conscientious, thoughtful, and honest? Or are you someone who leans on others, a "high-maintenance" friend who constantly needs to be told how much you are appreciated? What does your personal brand represent?

A Brand Evaluation

I believe that one of the biggest keys to getting what you want out of life is to believe so strongly in your own value that others believe in it, too. If you feel good about yourself, others will sign on to that belief. When you think of yourself as a product, it helps you see the importance of protecting your brand.

I first began building value for myself when I took up body-building. When I built myself up, I began carrying myself with more confidence, and as a result, I became more confident of my value as a person and, later, as a businessperson. Other people may build their brand value by obtaining college degrees or by learning technical, artistic, or athletic skills that increase their value in the marketplace. That value is determined by the guidelines you set for yourself, and whether or not you stay true to them over the course of your lifetime.

Why do some people lie on their résumés? Why do others cheat on their taxes, steal from their employers, abuse their loved ones, or otherwise engage in self-destructive and hurtful behavior? It is because they either have no values to guide them, or they have abandoned their values for some reason. If you establish values to guide your life and stick with them, you will rarely find yourself torn between doing what is right over the long term and doing what might just feel good in the short term.

So, what are the values I recommend that you follow? Well, it is up to you, really. We are all influenced by a unique combination of factors that determine which values we select or discard. In many cases, we inherit the values of our parents or those around us, but it is not all that rare for people to reject those inherited values and seek their own. It is also true that many people spend their life-times searching for the guiding light of values, and it is equally true that your values may shift throughout your lifetime.

Here are the primary values that I have established as my own guiding lights at this point in my life.

- *Integrity: I really am the guy I want you to think I am.* One night not long ago, Tracey and the kids and I were walking to our car from a restaurant near our home when three teenage girls wearing Domino's Pizza uniforms walked by. One of them spotted me and said, "You're Jake, aren't you? You are really cool, man."

  Having been a teenager once myself—hundreds of years ago—I realize how tough it can be for an adult to come across as "cool" to someone that age, so I really felt good about that little encounter. "I must be doing all right, if teenagers still think I'm cool," I thought.

The thing that I think I've done right is that I have never pretended to be anything other than what I am, a regular guy from Long Island. I don't think teenagers would buy in to me as a suave leading-man type, or as an East Coast Rambo. Obviously, they did buy in to me as Big Brother Jake, a regular sort of guy, because it fit me.

I'm not a naive person; I've been around show business too long for that. But I am still often amazed at the lack of honesty people practice in their everyday lives. To me, it is such a basic and vital principle. If you live honestly, if you don't pretend to be what you aren't, if you mean what you say and do what you promise, life is infinitely easier and more rewarding over the long term.

Now, I'm not perfect. (That may shock you, I know.) I've already told you about a couple of little fibs I served up. I couldn't ride a motorcycle when I was interviewing for the leader-of-the-pack role, so I wasn't exactly truthful, but I did *do* what they asked. I rode the motorcycle while somebody else pushed it. Hollywood is well stocked with people who pretend to be what they aren't. That is basically what acting is all about, isn't it? But believe it or not, I know many people here who have built successful careers on being honest, and on living up to their brand.

If you are a producer who completes a movie on time and within budget, chances are you will last longer in the entertainment industry than the guy who promises but does not deliver. If you are a carpenter who builds within the cost estimates you have given, you will do well. If you are a businessperson whose product or service lives up to the claims you make, chances are the customers will flock to you. If you are a husband or wife who deals honestly with your spouse, your marriage most likely will endure.

It is perhaps even more important that you be honest with *yourself*. My rule for living honestly is this: If you talk the talk, you have to walk the walk. I have made it a rule to do what I say I will do, and to be relentless in following through on my promises. As anyone who has ever done business with me knows, I expect the same of everyone I am associated with.

I want my brand, Body by Jake, to be viewed as a quality brand, one with integrity and value. And so that is how I try to live. How many people do you know who pretend to be one thing but are really something else? They pretend to be concerned about others, yet they always put their own concerns first. They pretend to be honest, but they don't do what they say they are going to do. That is definitely *not* the way to build brand value.

• *Optimism: I want to be a positive force not only in my life, but in the lives of everyone around me.*

It used to be that people who talked about being optimistic or positive were scoffed at for being naive Pollyannas by cynics and so-called sophisticated people. But behavioral scientists and psychologists now have scientific proof of the power of positive thinking. In the 1988 Summer Olympics, the U.S. swimmer Matt Biondi was expected to challenge the amazing performance of the former U.S. swimmer Mark Spitz, who in 1972 took seven gold medals. But in his first event, the 200-meter freestyle, Matt didn't live up to those high expectations. He finished third. In the next event, the 100-meter butterfly, he just missed winning the gold and finished second.

There was a lot of talk after those first two events that Matt would be so disappointed at finishing out of the gold in the early going that he might not get any gold medals at all. But there was one psychologist who knew that Matt was not the sort of person who would let past disappointments affect his future performance. That psychologist had conducted tests on Matt in the months prior to the Olympics. In written tests, the psychologist had found that Matt had a high degree of optimism.

In another test, the psychologist had Matt's swimming coach tell him during a big swimming event that he had finished his first heat with a much worse time than he had hoped. In truth, he had done very well, but the coach told

Matt that his time in the event was low and that he should try again. Even with the negative feedback and disappointment in his past performance, Matt went out and did even better than he had actually done before. The psychologist and the coach tried the same test with other swimmers who had taken written tests that showed them to have pessimistic attitudes, and they all did worse on their second attempts after being given negative feedback.

Other tests have found that students who score high as optimists also did better in the classroom, and that insurance salespeople who tested high as optimists sold 37 percent more insurance in their first two years than those who tested high as pessimists. In addition, the pessimistic insurance salespeople were twice as likely to become discouraged and quit during that period, according to these studies.

So you see, there is scientific proof that having an optimistic approach to life gives you an advantage. Living optimistically doesn't mean that you refuse to carry an umbrella when the sky is full of thunderclouds, or that you get on an airplane even though you see one of the engines is falling off. An optimist acknowledges challenges or danger, but she doesn't let them deter her from going after what she wants. The optimist knows that there will be failures in life, but unlike the pessimist, the optimist views failure as a temporary condition.

This positive approach to life springs from a belief in your own ability to control your life and to deal with life's challenges. That positive belief in yourself makes you more willing to take risks and to go after goals. When you are optimistic about your ability to achieve your goals, it has a positive impact on your performance. Rather than worrying about what might go wrong, you go after what you want with the sense that you can handle anything that life throws at you.

When other people see you as someone who takes a positive approach, they are drawn to you. They want to plug in to that positive energy, and so they come to you with ideas and opportunities. They believe in you because they sense that you believe in yourself. I have seen this work time and time again in my businesses. When advertisers for my *Body by Jake* magazine saw that I believed in my product and that I was determined to make it a success, they decided to buy in to it too. If I had approached them with an attitude that said, "Well, we're not sure this is going to work but we want you to take a chance on us," I don't think they would have bought a cup of coffee from me, let alone a full-page color ad. Do you?

- *Balance: I am the sum of many parts, and the most important thing to me is to remain balanced in all that I do and believe in.*

   I know actors who have given their lives to their careers and won the highest awards, and have been miserable human beings. I've known people with incredible wealth who have said they would trade it all to be able to spend their evenings on the living room floor playing with their children. What do these unhappy and unfulfilled people have in common? A lack of balance.

   I probably work harder at achieving balance than at any other aspect of my life. Every day, every week, every year, I walk away from work to spend time with my family because I don't want to lose my balance. In my business enterprises, I have pursued opportunities in marketing, television and movies, publishing, and scores of other arenas because I believe you need balance there too.

   When you approach life from a balanced perspective, it becomes very difficult for anything to knock you off track. Preserving balance builds your brand value because people believe they can come to you and present you with challenges and opportunities. The balanced person isn't thrown off when encountering challenges in one aspect of life because the overall quality of his or her existence is so strong. A bad day at the office means only that I am more eager to go home and enjoy my wife and children. Having balance in my life makes my brand stronger. It is one of my most useful and rewarding brand values.

Once you have decided what values you will live by, you will always have a built-in compass to keep you on your chosen course. What values guided me in making that decision even before I talked to Steve Ross? Certainly my desire to live up to my image as a believer in a healthy lifestyle. My optimistic approach fit in here, too, because I didn't fall into the trap of thinking that if I passed up this opportunity there might not be any others. As a positive-minded person, I *knew* there would be other and better opportunities down the road. And finally, it was my resolve to remain balanced that helped me see that rather than grabbing for the money, I should think about the possible long-term implications. My values keep me on track as I build and expand my brand. When things get cloudy or confusing, my values show me the way.

Brand Building 101

Follow these steps to help identify your values and the rules for fulfilling them in order to build your brand.

1. List the values you believe are most important to you now and over the course of your entire life.

   Here are examples: love, happiness, wealth, power, continuous growth, laughter, intellectual stimulation, giving to others, success, optimism, integrity, balance, recognition.
2. Rank each of the values that you came up with in their order of importance to you. (Take your time. This is not a race.)
3. Take each of the values as you have ranked them and write a paragraph explaining what has to happen to make you feel that those values have been attained in your life. For example, if you ranked happiness as a top value, what will it take to make you feel happy? What will it take to make you feel intellectually stimulated? Successful? Balanced?
4. Now, study the "rules" that you have created for your value system. Have you made it easy or difficult to attain the values that you think are important? For example, will it take a million dollars in your savings account to make you feel like

a successful person, or will you feel successful if you can build a number of loving and supporting relationships?

You see, it isn't just the *values* you select that are important, it is the *rules* you create for satisfying those values that really impact your life. If you don't feel that you will ever be successful until you have a million dollars in the bank, that puts a lot of pressure on you, and maybe it is far too narrow a rule for success. It might be better to say that you will allow yourself to feel successful when you are involved in fulfilling work and rewarding relationships and you are able to comfortably support yourself and those who depend on you.

I can't choose your value system for you. It is up to you to build your brand. I can only give you a process and urge you to think carefully about building your brand and how you choose to live your life. Often, people have problems not because their values are wrong, but because the rules they create for fulfilling them are wrong.

Have you ever had a "high-maintenance" friend, someone whom you could never seem to please or who always seemed to get angry or hurt at the slightest things? Chances are that this person really does want to have close relationships—in fact, he or she may be desperate for just that. But even though they value friendships, their rules for what a friendship must be are unrealistic. If you asked one of these people to write down what someone must do to be a true friend, the list might read something like this:

- A true friend must always put my needs first.
- A true friend always agrees with me, even when I might be wrong.
- A true friend would never do anything without including me.
- A true friend never gets angry or upset with me, no matter what I might do.

Do you see the challenge here? The high-maintenance friend has established rules that almost guarantee any relationship will fall short of what he or she demands of it. Very few people would be willing to stay involved in a friendship that demands so much and gives so little. Yet I'll bet you have run into a high-maintenance person whose rules are similar to this. You may even have your own set of poorly conceived and self-destructive rules built into your own value system. For example, make a list of what it takes to make you happy. Have you ever seriously thought about it? Do you consider yourself a happy person? Or is it difficult to make you happy? This is no small issue, by the way. Aristotle, as well as many modern-day psychologists, believed that much of what we do in life is motivated by our pursuit of the state of mind we describe as happiness. We may value success, or friendships, or love because we think it will make us happy, but don't we want happiness just for its own sake?

If your rules for being happy require that everyone like you and agree with you, that you have no concerns about money, that your relationships all be perfect, and that there not be a single weed in your garden—well, then, you have set yourself up for *unhappiness,* haven't you? Now, let's redraw those rules. What if all it takes to make you happy is that you have people who care about you and a job that helps better the lives of others? Those rules make it a whole lot easier to be happy, don't they?

What if the high-maintenance friend decides to change the rules that he or she has established for friendships? The new rules say this: "From now on, my friends don't have to do anything other than occasionally spend some time with me talking about *their* lives." Suddenly, our high-maintenance friend has become low-maintenance. And in the process, it becomes a lot easier for the value of friendship to be fulfilled, doesn't it?

If you want to build values into your brand, it is vital that you put just as much thought into designing the rules that you create for fulfilling those values as you do for choosing the values. If you do this carefully, you can make it a whole lot easier for yourself, and for those around you, to live a dynamic and fulfilling life as a quality brand.

Protecting Your Brand

Even after you have established the values and principles that you have chosen to guide your life, you still must establish your brand;

you have to *live* according to those values and principles, and you must protect your brand as your most prized possession, because that is exactly what it is.

Nobody is going to be more concerned about protecting your brand than you. The more successful you become, the more important it is to guard the value of your name, both in the marketplace, where it relates to your career or business, and in your relationships, where it impacts the quality of your life and the lives of the people you care the most about. How do you protect your brand value as an individual? Never sell out, and never allow anyone else to tempt you into diminishing the quality of your brand.

I know of a guy whose first job out of college was as a "Coke spy." He was an undercover agent for Coca-Cola and his job was to drive around the southeastern United States visiting drive-ins, fast-food joints, fine restaurants, sports stadiums, anyplace that sold soft drinks in cups and glasses rather than cans and bottles. He would go into these places, order a Coke, and when the waitress or waiter wasn't looking, pour some of it into a container hidden under his shirt or jacket. Later, he would mark on the container where and when he had gathered the sample; then he would send it off to Coca-Cola's laboratory to be tested.

At the lab, Coca-Cola's analysts would determine whether the drink given to their Coke spy was in fact Coca-Cola or some other soft-drink product such as Pepsi or RC. If it turned out that the business was presenting someone else's cola as Coke, then Coca-Cola's legal department would send a "cease and desist" letter to the business, ordering them to make it clear to their patrons exactly what they were getting. Obviously, Coca-Cola, one of the best-run companies in the world for more than one hundred years, understands the importance of protecting its brand.

Your Lifelong Mission Is to Expand the Brand

I look at protecting and expanding my brand as a lifelong mission. In my business, not only am I always looking for ways to enhance the quality of what we do and to "expand the brand," I am also on my guard to make sure that neither I nor any of my employees gets Body by Jake's brand name involved in something that could diminish its value. I've been a fanatic about that since I first got involved in my personal training business in Hollywood.

I was able to build a clientele that included not only the top stars and most influential entertainment industry executives, but also other major business figures because they bought in to my brand. They believed that my brand could add value to their lives. When I did that for them, they helped me expand my brand beyond my wildest dreams.

I'll let you in on a little secret here. I never advertised my personal training business. I didn't have business cards or even a listed telephone number. My new clients had to *find* me by finding out who my existing clients were and getting my telephone number from them. My brand was so strong that they were willing to make that kind of effort.

My personal training business had established high standards for all of the others who came after me. As I expanded my brand, I made sure we maintained those high standards. We were particularly cautious when we entered the infomercial market because, in its early stages, that market featured a lot of shoddy merchandise and silly gadgets. I'd like to think that we helped elevate the infomercial industry by producing high-quality shows featuring high-quality products. We didn't present anything that wouldn't do what we claimed it could. We were simply protecting the value of our Body by Jake brand, and in doing that we encouraged other brand-conscious entrepreneurs and businesspeople to get into the infomercial market.

In my personal life, expanding the value of my brand involves deciding what I value most and setting high standards and principles for the way I live. Having children is a great responsibility, a wonderful addition to my life, and a reality check on how I approach life. If you don't practice what you preach, your children have no qualms about calling you on it. They are also mirrors of your actions. They take their attitudes and approaches from how they see their parents acting and interacting with other people.

If you want your children to respect you and to grow up as self-assured, responsible, and happy people, you first have to provide them with a model for that. You are their brand model. If you live up to the standards that you have set, then the odds are great that they will too.

To practice PowerLiving, you must create a brand built on values and principles that hold you to high standards. The most important of all of these values is that while you build and expand your brand, you also enhance the lives of those around you!

POWERLIVING
LESSON NO. 7

Success Is a Decision

In early 1992, I nearly threw one of our equipment-manufacturing partners out a window for suggesting that we try marketing Body by Jake fitness products on television with infomercials.

"Infomercials! Are you kidding me? Haven't I lectured you about the importance of protecting our brand? I'm not going to market my high-quality products on late-night television along with those knives that cut through steel, the fishing pole that fits into your pants pocket, and the Veg-A-Whatchamacallit that slices, dices, and plays 'The Star Spangled Banner.' Infomercials, in-SCHMO-mercials! Get outta here!"

Okay, so I overreacted a little. At that point, infomercials were still considered the flea market of television. The quality of the products they pushed was only slightly worse than the quality of the production, which generally looked like the shows had been shot in someone's garage off an alley in Brooklyn.

I was absolutely dead set against selling Body by Jake products on infomercials until Phil Scotti, the president of my company, explained to me how we could develop our own breakthrough high-quality infomercials to sell our high-quality products and expand our brand. Phil had the vision that infomercials, if done properly, could drive retail and home shopping sales. I was willing to give this new marketing tool a try *if* I could elevate the infomercial to match the quality of our products and the value of our brand.

Our first thirty-minute infomercial was produced in partnership with USA Direct, an infomercial company, in 1992. It featured our FirmFlex, the first home fitness machine designed to work the whole body without the use of weight stacks. It provided a complete workout with seven exercises, which we called "the Simple Seven," that can be done in twenty minutes every day. We sold over 600,000 FirmFlex machines with that infomercial, and the FirmFlex became the top-selling home fitness machine in the country, with a 98 percent customer satisfaction rating. Our business took a major leap forward as a result of that first infomercial. The decision to try the infomercial format radically changed our business and our lives.

That first infomercial's success put us in a position to negotiate a very strong deal with our infomercial partner, which was eager to sign my company to a long-term contract. It is important to note here that infomercials are generally considered a very high-risk marketing tool. It costs at least $150,000 to produce a good infomercial and hundreds of thousands more to buy the television time, which has become more and more expensive. On top of that, about nine out of ten infomercials don't make it out of the testing phase.

That is a risky business, and even though our first infomercial had done incredibly well, I wasn't at all certain that we could repeat that success every time we went on the air with a new product. As I mentioned in the previous chapter, I am always looking to expand the brand by pushing the envelope and seeing what new peaks we can conquer. Earlier in my business career, though, I had a tendency to want to *capture* success, to own it and never let it get away. You really can't do that. In the case of the infomercial deal, we decided to negotiate a five-year contract. We made that decision thoughtfully, but we made it essentially out of fear, and believe me, any decision made out of fear is the wrong decision.

I was afraid that the enormous success of the first infomercial was a "Vanilla Ice." Do you remember Vanilla Ice? . . . See what I mean? He made a major splash in the music industry, and then quickly sank out of sight. You hear about these one-hit wonders all the time in the entertainment business and in business in general.

Out of fear of being a one-hit wonder in the infomercial business, and out of a desire for security over the long term, I negotiated a very lucrative five-year deal to do more infomercials. Everyone had told us how incredible our first success was, and I made the decision to do the five-year deal in order to protect myself and our business in case the next infomercial didn't work. I thought that was a wise decision, and all of my Go-To People agreed.

Well, our second infomercial introduced the Body by Jake Hip and Thigh Machine to the American public, and they responded by buying even more of them than of the FirmFlex. We followed that amazing success with a third infomercial, this one for the Body by Jake Ab and Back Plus. It won Infomercial of the Year, Best Infomercial Product, and Best Product Offer awards from NIMA, the National Infomercial Marketing Association.

Those three infomercials did over $250 million in gross sales, and all three were the top-selling infomercials of their years. Those three infomercials each grossed more than 95 percent of the feature films made in the same time frame. When I realized that, I called my pal Wiels and told him he was in the wrong business. He said he was proud of me. He likes it when I try to keep him humble.

In spite of the success of our infomercials, I was feeling pretty humble myself. Although I had thought it was a wise decision at the time, I should not have tied myself to a five-year contract with our infomercial partner. Why? We made more money than we had ever dreamed of from those infomercials, but we undoubtedly would have made even more if I had been able to renegotiate our deal with our partner after each infomercial was made. Instead, my company was locked in to a five-year deal that, while very lucrative, did not allow us to fully capitalize on our successes. The long-term contract tied us to one company. Based on our successes, we could have played the field and taken the best offer.

Signing the five-year deal was not the result of a bad decision or a deadly decision. It was not a roll-up-the-tents-and-go-home-and-cry decision. I played the odds that said infomercials are a high-risk undertaking and one huge initial success is no guarantee of future success. I was looking out for the long-term life of my brand based on the history of the infomercial business. What I did not foresee was that our high-quality products would lead to a major shift in the industry. Our success helped make infomercials a far more respectable marketing tool.

The decision was well considered and appeared to be a smart and a thoughtful move at the time, and still it cost us a bundle of money. After the successes of the Hip and Thigh Machine and the Ab and Back Plus, I felt a bit like the guy who fell in love with a luxury car, signed a five-year lease, then after a couple years saw another model that he really liked a lot more. I couldn't make a move because I had tied myself to a long-term deal.

We made a decision we later regretted, but I do not regret making the decision. Does that sound confusing? Well, what I mean is that if we had made our decision to sign the five-year deal without giving it careful consideration or without thinking through every aspect of it, I would have been seriously upset. But the truth is, we made a good decision based on the information we had at the time. The problem was, we made it out of a fear of failure rather than out of the drive to succeed.

Quality Decisions Mean a Quality Life

Success *is* a decision. You and you alone decide whether or not you are going to relentlessly pursue success, and the decisions you make along the way determine how successful you become. Every action you take in your life, for better or for worse, begins with a decision.

Consider some of the crucial decisions we make in our lives:

- We decide what to do for a living.
- We decide whom to spend our lives with.
- We decide where to live.
- We decide what is an acceptable comfort level.

Whether it involves picking a business partner or a marriage partner, selecting a career or a college, the quality of your decisions determines the level of success you achieve in every aspect of your life. If you are happy living in a log cabin in the woods, that is your decision. If you decide that it will take a mansion in Connecticut to make you comfortable, then you will undoubtedly strive to get it. Your decisions set the standards for your life.

Some people never move forward with their lives because they don't understand the difference between making a *decision* and making a *wish*. When you make a decision, you commit to taking an action that propels you forward. You leave all other options behind. When you make a wish, you are not committing to taking an action, so you remain stationary. A wish changes nothing. A decision changes *everything*.

Take a minute to think about some of the important decisions you have made. Write down how each of them changed your life in a way that was either beneficial or detrimental to your success. Don't second-guess yourself while doing this, but *do* consider just how important the decisions you have made have been, and how much they have impacted your life.

Taking Decisive Action

When I look at many of the successful people I know, it strikes me time and time again that a great many of them, from Steven Spielberg to Bette Midler to Harrison Ford to Steve Ross, came from unremarkable and sometimes difficult backgrounds. It wasn't their circumstances that made them successful; it was the decisions they made along the way that made each of their lives truly remarkable. Wiels was a kid from a troubled family who *decided* to rise above his circumstances and chase his dream of making movies. Bette grew up in a trailer park, but she *decided* that she could create a better life by entertaining people. Harrison Ford flunked out of a small Wisconsin college and had to support his family as a carpenter, but he *decided* that he could be a successful actor, and he was right. Steve Ross came from a poor family in the Flatbush district of Brooklyn, his father lost a successful business in the Depression and never recovered, but all of his life Steve made *decisions* that made him successful beyond his wildest dreams.

These people have nothing on you. They simply tapped into their power to decide not to focus on their circumstances or backgrounds and instead to focus on the lives they wanted to create for themselves. You and I have the power to make the decisions that will change our lives, too. It is probably the greatest gift we have.

You first have to learn to trust and believe in that power, and then you have to understand how to make good decisions. Note that I said *good* decisions. Your power to make decisions is a double-edged sword because you have the power to make bad decisions too. You can decide to change your life for the better, or you can decide to settle for what you have. You can decide to move to a higher level in your career by pursuing an advanced degree or you can decide that you really aren't all that unhappy with what you have now, which is okay too.

You can decide to get out of an unhappy relationship, or you can decide that you would rather stick with what you have than make the effort to change. It is up to you to make the right decision for you. I can't do that, but I can show you how to make decisions wisely.

The challenge for most people is that they do not have a regular *conscious process* for making important decisions. Instead, they make their important decisions in much the same way they decide what shirt to wear or what breakfast cereal to eat—*unconsciously.* If you haven't been getting what you want out of life, chances are that you have been living according to unconscious decisions. Rather than setting goals and creating a plan to go after those goals, you have simply let life sweep you along. Of course, that way of living is the result of an unconscious decision you made to simply drift along like a person in a motorboat who is too lazy or unmotivated to start the engine. If you are not happy with the results that drifting has brought you, if you find yourself going where you really don't want to go, or if you are simply stuck in a whirlpool and can't get free, then you have to make a conscious decision to start the motor.

If you want more out of life, you cannot make important decisions on autopilot. You have to put careful thought into decisions that might affect the rest of your life: decisions on what career to choose, which opportunities to pursue, and whom you want to spend your life with. Those are key decisions that can have a major impact on whether you practice PowerLiving!

Deciding Factors

The challenge is that we make so many minor decisions each day that we don't always adjust our decision-making process when it comes time to make the really difficult decisions, such as "Should I go back for my master's degree or look for a new job?" or "Should I give up the guaranteed paycheck in my current job in order to start my own business?" or "Should I buy the luxury car as a way of building a successful image, or should I save my money for more practical things?"

These are all difficult decisions that require careful consideration. But most people don't have a process for making decisions thoughtfully and carefully. Do you know how to make good decisions? First try making a few really bad ones. No kidding, I had never given a lot of thought to developing a serious process for making decisions until I made some whoppers.

When you are young and just getting started, you don't have a lot to lose, so your bad decisions don't hurt that much. Usually you don't have a family or a mortgage or a reputation to protect in the early going. But let me tell you, once you acquire a few of those things, it gets a lot more serious, and that is when you have to start thinking hard about how you make your decisions. As a body-builder, I learned that it isn't necessarily how much weight you lift that is important, it is how many *repetitions* you do at that weight. That is how muscle mass is built. The same holds true with your decision-making strength. The more decisions you make, the stronger your decision-making powers will become.

Will you make bad decisions? Almost certainly. Why? Because no one can predict the future. What may look like a great decision one day could turn out to be disastrous the next. It is important, then, to make *thoughtful* decisions, so that even if the ones you make occasionally go sour, you will know that at the very least, you made it fully understanding both the potential rewards and risks.

Here are the Deciding Factors you should consider in making important decisions.

1. *Measure the decision against your Ultimate Goal.*

   Before I take action on a decision, I hold it up to the light of my Ultimate Goal to see how it aligns with my long-term and short-term goals. Does it move me five steps closer, or does it move me laterally or away from the Ultimate Goal? Is it a move that I am making just for the sake of making a move or is it a major step forward?

   I've found it is wise as a first step to check how each decision fits into your plan for your life. To do this, use your imagination to examine the impact on your life of the decision made both ways. "If I make the decision to sign the long-term infomercial contract, what impact will it have on my goals to build my business and to provide for my family? How will it impact my brand?"

   I made some poor decisions a few years ago when I tried to expand my brand by opening a Body by Jake fitness studio in New York City. I wasn't as careful or thoughtful as I should have been in choosing a partner to run the studio for me and I got too excited and ambitious in selecting a location for the studio. I always want to do things in a big way and a classy manner, so I decided to locate the studio in midtown Manhattan. The rent was double what we budgeted. It made a big splash at first, but then I had some real challenges in dealing with my partner. So I decided to close it. On the brighter side, it made me think a lot harder about the process of making decisions.

2. *Evaluate the benefits and the risks.*

   It never hurts to sit down with pencil and paper and write down all the positive results that can come of a decision in one column and all of the negative results in another. If you discover that the negative side fills up a lot quicker than the positive side, then you probably ought to bail out. It's not always so crystal clear at the beginning, though, and sometimes you may have to get pretty far down the road in evaluating the decision before it becomes apparent to you one way or another.

When I make a decision, I carefully weigh the pros and cons. I make a list showing all of the possible benefits and all of the potential challenges. I envision myself making the decision first one way and then the other. I play it out in my mind in order both to prepare myself and to try and foresee what might develop as a result of the decision. This reality check is particularly important when you are considering taking an action that seems especially attractive and appealing.

If you had happened to be hanging around the fabulous Bel Air Hotel one afternoon last year, you might have witnessed a curious sight, even for that legendary inn. Had you kept your eye on the door, you might have seen an unprecedented meeting of the minds and the muscles when I brought together the leading fitness advocates in the country: Kathy Smith, Tamilee Webb, Jack LaLanne, and Richard Simmons. (Jane Fonda sent her regrets.) I had called them together not to compare calves and abs but to consider a business proposal. I had several other friends who were involved in highly successful and lucrative theme-restaurant ventures, including the Hard Rock Cafe, the House of Blues, and Planet Hollywood. In talks with these friends about their operations, it was suggested that I should consider my own theme restaurant chain based on healthy foods. (No "Hamburger Buns of Steel" jokes, please.)

The more I thought about that suggestion, the more I liked it. It made sense. The American public was becoming more and more conscious about eating healthy foods and the fitness industry was rocking with a group of very high-profile and savvy ambassadors. I had contacted each of them and they all were enthusiastic. Even Jane Fonda loved the idea, but she said that she was devoting more time to her private life.

It was difficult to get so many busy folks together, but we finally convened at the Bel Air for a day of discussion of the

concept. In the previous chapter, I told you about the benefits of operating out of an abundance mentality in which you
believe there is enough success out there for everybody, and
this meeting was a great example. We all are in the health
and fitness business, but each understood that there was
room for all. Everyone in attendance agreed that the restaurant concept would be beneficial to us individually and col-
lectively.

The name we came up with for the restaurant was Eden
because we wanted it to be a little bit of heaven on earth—
a place where you could eat all you wanted without the
usual side order of guilt. The challenge was that we didn't
want to restrict the menu to "health food"; instead, we decided to offer a wide variety of foods in their healthiest
forms. We would have hamburgers, but they would be lean
beef. We would have cheese, but it would be low-fat. The
chicken would be rotisserie rather than fried, and even the
pizzas would be light on calories and fat. We would offer
desserts too, because I always allow myself one day of the
week, usually Saturdays, to eat anything I want. We were
going to incorporate that idea into the menu by proclaim-
ing, "Every day is Saturday."

Once all of my fit friends signed on to that basic concept,
it was decided that I would meet with the major restaurant
consulting firms in the country and present the idea to them.
I would get their reactions and solicit their bids to manage
Eden for us, and report back to the entire group of investors.
Over the next six months, I met with a half dozen of the consulting firms and we eventually whittled it down to a decision between two of them. But before we voted on which
one we wanted to lead our restaurant chain, we made another important decision. We decided to put Eden on hold.

The idea is not dead by any means, but after we had
looked at the figures and considered most of the major aspects of the restaurant business, we concluded that the
smartest decision was to pull back and think about this for a
while. Part of the challenge was that each of us is already in-

volved in so many enterprises that demand so much of our time. It was difficult for any of us to put aside adequate time to learn about this new business. Another sticking point was the fact that each of the participants is involved in lucrative licensing and merchandising deals and there were all sorts of questions as to how we would each protect our individual brands while also licensing and marketing products in the joint venture.

After we had worked on this for more than a year, we realized that we still had more questions than answers, and that is usually a good indication that the best decision is to put the deal on hold. Let me suggest to you one Golden Rule of Decision Making: If it is taking you too long to decide, then decide not to decide and look for other opportunities.

I am comfortable with what we did in the Eden venture because we made the decision carefully and thoughtfully, and so I consider it a success *as a decision* as well as a success from a business point of view. We evaluated the upsides and downsides, the potential benefits and risks, and we decided that, at that particular time, there were too many questions that we could not answer.

3. *Go with your gut and get on with it.*

After you have checked the decision against your Ultimate Goal and studied the potential benefits and risks, if you still don't have overwhelming evidence one way or the other, my advice is to go with your instincts. If you do what your heart tells you, you may not always make the right move, but you will be able to live with yourself. The *worst* thing you can do is simply not make a decision. As I mentioned earlier, the only way to learn to make good decisions is to practice your decision-making skills. I'm a big believer in going with my gut feelings because that policy has generally served me well over the years. I had questions about the infomercial business, but my president, Phil Scotti, made me feel better about it, and after listening to him I decided to go with it. My gut instincts were wrong when it came to selecting the partner in the New York studio.

Generally, when I go with a gut decision, it is only after I've made sure that even if it turns out to be wrong, there is always a backup plan to put into action. I refuse to take a leap without a net. I think that is foolish and irresponsible, particularly if other people are counting on you. Back in the days before I was doing infomercials, when I was trying to grow Body by Jake from a small but high-profile fitness training business into a multifaceted multi-media company, we tried to think big—bigger than our bank accounts. Our plan at the time was to license our brand name to fitness centers in hotels, country clubs, and other locations around the country. The goal was to have Body by Jake boutiques in these locations to sell clothing, videos, and fitness equipment.

We had a great marketing campaign in which we tried to leverage my image as the Trainer to the Stars into something far more substantial. We sent the CEOs of all the major hotel chains, spas, and private clubs a very fancy invitation. "You are invited to join Steven Spielberg, Harrison Ford, Bette Midler, and Morgan Fairchild as clients of Body by Jake" was the message on the box.

People loved the concept. They were all for it. But none were willing to pay the tab. It was the early 1990s, a time of tight money, particularly for the hotel industry. It became clear that if we were going to spin our way into a big business, we needed to find our own financing. We looked at a number of methods for acquiring the cash we needed. We talked to bankers and private investors and venture capitalists and a whole parade of people. It was like a bad movie populated by bizarre characters and wheeler-dealers. Nothing worked out, primarily because we had very little leverage. I didn't have a college education or a business degree, and while I was making more money than I had ever made in my life, it wasn't enough to make your typical Beverly Hills banker dig deep into his pockets.

After a year of searching for financing, I was getting frustrated. Tracey and I had just gotten married and I was eager to get my business on track. We were talking about my frustration one night when she got that determined look in her eyes and said, "What about taking out a second mortgage on the house?"

I nearly fell out of my chair. "You would risk losing the house?" I asked.

"Hey, I believe in you."

I am a lucky guy, and I believe in myself, but I don't think I ever would have thought of putting our first house on the line. We loved that house. We had been in it only seven or eight months. It had a lot of open space for entertaining people, and a great yard. It had been more than we could afford, but we'd fallen in love with it.

Tracey and I talked for days about her proposal, and in the end, we concluded that it was a good idea. We didn't have any children yet. We were both working. If the very worst-case scenario happened and we had to give up the house, we could always go live in my car on the beach. In the end, Tracey made the point that we had to believe in ourselves and our dreams and go after them before we could expect anybody else to buy in to them. Tracey has a business background and she is a smart lady—as well as a great judge of character, I might add.

Still, taking out a second mortgage was a scary thing to do. You don't do something like that without giving it a great deal of thought. But it was a risk I figured I had to take in order to make a major move from being a guy with a personal training business to becoming a businessman in the fitness field.

It was a big decision, but we felt it was an investment in our future. I believe also that at the end of my life I want to be able to look back and say that I practiced PowerLiving, that I forged my own path instead of sticking to the safe and proven one.

Breaking Away

Throughout your climb toward your Ultimate Goal, there will come critical points when the step-by-step approach just won't cut it. Such a point will generally come immediately after you have picked up momentum by reaching a level of success that you have been trying to attain for a long time, or it might follow an unexpected success. You need to learn to recognize these times and to prepare for them so that when the opportunity arises, you can make a breakaway that will move you much further ahead than you might have anticipated.

In the *Star Wars* movies, Han Solo and company repeatedly leave their galactic foes in the cosmic dust by "going to light speed." *That* is what it feels like to make a breakaway. You may think you are cruising along just fine, slowly picking up speed, but every now and then you'll have a chance to make a huge leap ahead by going to light speed. This almost always involves taking what you will perceive as a risk. I prefer to think of it as a *breakaway opportunity* to take that momentum and do something momentous.

The best time to take a risk is when you have momentum, just as the best time to jump across a stream is when you've built up speed. You shouldn't take risks because you are desperate not to fail; you should take them because you are hungry to succeed. I had tasted considerable success with my personal training business, and that made me hungry for more success. I wanted to keep that momentum flowing. I wanted to use it to build a more substantial foundation as a businessman. I had taken small steps to get the personal training business going, and it had taken off. I was ready to make a breakaway, and if I had to take a calculated risk to do it, I was ready.

I believe that taking risks is the only way to grow and to create a dynamic, entrepreneurial lifestyle. That does not mean that you take unwise risks or ill-considered risks. It means that some risks are absolutely worth taking and that you need to carefully evaluate each risk as it is presented.

How do you evaluate risk? You make sure that even if you fail and you lose all that you have invested, you still have options—not to mention a place to sleep. You also don't take risks that might destroy your reputation or make it impossible for you to resume your journey toward the Ultimate Goal. And, finally, you don't take risks for the wrong reason: for ego. Here are things you should consider when evaluating risks.

1. *What has brought you to the risk?*

    If the risk was a gap between two mountains, what would have brought you to it? Were you running *after* something or *away from* something? Does the risk stand between you and something you want? Or is your motivation to put something behind you? In other words, are you fleeing from pain or toward pleasure?

It is perfectly acceptable to take risks because you want more for your life, as long as you understand that it is not taking the risk that changes your life, it is the continuous pursuit of goals and dreams that does that.

2. *What is it exactly that you want to accomplish by taking this risk?*

   Just as you wouldn't jump blindly off a building without knowing where you intend to land, you shouldn't take risks without understanding exactly what you intend to accomplish. I would never have taken out a second mortgage just to get my hands on some extra cash unless it was for something absolutely essential. I wouldn't use it to buy a nicer car. That would have been foolish. But if that money could help me grow my business and in the long run enhance our financial security, then it was a risk worth taking.

3. *Review the opportunities that will be created both if you should fail and if you should succeed.*

   It is important to understand that even if you fail when you have taken a risk, you will create new opportunities, and opportunities are all you need to restore your momentum. You should always have a plan of action prepared for either failure or success. Work the scenarios out so that if you land on your feet, you can hit the ground running, and if you land on your back or your head, you can roll up and return to your feet quickly to look for the next opportunity.

   Not every risk will work—that's the nature of the game— but there should be an opportunity to grow, whether or not the risk works out as you had hoped. If you understand that, and prepare yourself to move on immediately, you will greatly reduce your lost time and effort.

   If Tracey and I had not committed to taking out that second mortgage and then devoting ourselves to using the additional money to create greater success for our business, then why do it at all? As it turned out, that additional money helped finance our move into infomercials, which allowed us to pay off the first house and buy an even nicer one.

4. *Acknowledge the joy that comes with taking risks, with growing, and with living life to its fullest.*

I've taken so many risks I'm surprised I can get insurance. I enjoy pushing the envelope, it is part of my nature. I have already exceeded every expectation. When you don't put any limits on yourself, when you tend to believe that *anything* is possible, then you welcome risk as a way to expand your dream.

A Breakaway Break

One of the more enjoyable risks I have taken in recent years was on a football field in front of 80,000 fans. No, I didn't decide to become Troy Aikman for a day. My company has worked with the National Football League over the years in developing a motivational fitness program for young people, and a few years ago, we decided to try doing an "NFL fitness break" between the third and fourth quarters at a game between the Kansas City Chiefs and the Los Angeles Rams. The idea was to promote the fitness break as football's answer to baseball's seventh-inning stretch. Now the risks in this were fairly high. There were 80,000 people out there, and I could have made a fool of myself. Driving to Kansas City's Arrowhead Stadium on the day of the game, I was with one of the guys with NFL Properties and Phil Scotti, president of Body by Jake. I was getting psyched up and I told the guy from NFL Properties that two things could go wrong. By the third quarter the Chiefs could be losing. He said, "Jake, they are playing the Rams. The Chiefs have won their first three games. The Rams have lost theirs." Then, although I am not a downer guy, I said, "Well, it could rain."

"Naw," he said. "There isn't a cloud in the sky and there is no rain in the forecast."

Cut to ten seconds remaining in the third quarter. I am standing under a tarp with those two guys and the Kansas City marching band. I am wearing two microphones; one from NFL Films, one for the stadium. I am exasperated. It is *pouring* rain, and the Chiefs are losing 17–zip.

Things are looking bleak. The guy from NFL Properties leans over and whispers to me, "You don't have to do this if you don't want to."

But they had been promoting Body by Jake all during the game on the JumboTron giant video screen, so there was no way I was going to quit.

"I'm in," I said.

When the gun sounded for the end of the third quarter I sprinted out on the field. The Kansas City cheerleaders joined me and together we led 80,000 rain-soaked and roaring fans in the world's first NFL fitness break. When we were finished with the exercise routine, I yelled for everybody to scream "Touchdown!" and the roar they put out shook the entire state. I got such a rush you would have thought that I had scored a touchdown myself. It was amazing.

I'll never forget the cheers and laughter of all those people standing in their soaked clothes and rain gear, jumping up and down. At one point, I looked up at the giant video screen at the end of the stadium, and there was *my* face, magnified to the size of a three-story building. And do you know what? The response of the crowd convinced me that this risk had been worth it!

POWERLIVING
LESSON NO. 8

Face Your Fears

Recently I did something that at one time frightened me more than watching *Dracula* in the dark, more than strange sounds going bump in the night, even more than asking the lovely Barbara Sivin to go steady in sixth grade.

I stood in front of several thousand people and gave a speech.

You may think that would not be such a big deal for a guy who has made hundreds of personal appearances, been on network television countless times, and had his face magnified to the size of a department store on the Kansas City Chiefs' scoreboard screen.

This was different.

This speaking appearance forced me once again to face the Big One, my greatest fear: The Return of the Stutter.

I had been invited to give a speech to an audience of hundreds of people who stuttered just as I once had. If you have never stuttered, you cannot comprehend what it is like to be a stutterer, or a former stutterer, in this situation. To have this challenge of being a stutterer as a child, when you are so vulnerable to the opinions of other kids, is traumatic. That childhood trauma never really goes away.

I was a gregarious kid and it should have been the most natural thing in the world for me to stand up in front of my classmates and answer the teacher's questions or read aloud. Instead, those simple acts were nightmares.

The fear of having to recite in class was worse than the actual act of doing it, which is typical of the fears that we create in our minds. Fear is nothing more than our brain alerting us to *be prepared*. Unfortunately, we give fear more meaning than that. There is an ancient story in Eastern philosophy about a wise man sitting underneath a tree near a road when the Spirit of the Plague passes by. The wise man asks the Spirit of the Plague where it is headed and it replies, "I am going to the city, where I shall slay one hundred persons."

Months later, the Spirit of the Plague returns and the wise man again hails it. "You told me that you were only going to kill one hundred people, but I've heard that ten thousand died."

Replied the Spirit of the Plague, "I killed only one hundred. Fear killed the others."

Fear is a mere emotion, simply a message from the brain to our bodies to get prepared for action. Often as children we give our fears real power over our lives and our dreams. If we buy in to our fears, we give them power over us by creating monsters. As adults we do the same thing. We take our fears of rejection, of criticism, or of responsibility and we invest those fears with real power by creating monsters to go with them.

Do you know people who take offense at the slightest thing? Do you know people who need to be constantly told how much they are appreciated? These are people who have allowed their fears and insecurities to dominate their lives. They fear the monsters of rejection and disapproval, and so they constantly demand acceptance and approval. Their lives are thrown off balance by their fears. Some may fear criticism to the point that they don't express their true beliefs or act upon them. Some fear loneliness, so they enter into unhealthy relationships. Others have such a fear of death that every minor ailment becomes a deadly disease.

Too often we allow our fears to control our actions, instead of taking action to get beyond our fears. I'm sure you know people who have never dared to go after what they want in life because they were afraid of rejection or failure. Fear cripples people, and it stunts lives. Facing your fears is a key element in PowerLiving.

I was about fifteen years old when my father announced to the family that he was going to quit his job selling insurance and start his own business. He said we were going to have to tighten our belts while he made the switch. He took a year off and put together a magazine to be distributed to real estate agencies around the country. It was a magazine that businesses could give away to people moving into a town. My father did very well with that magazine business.

I was a little scared at the time, although probably not as scared as my parents. But I admired my dad for having the guts to go after what he wanted for his life. Here was a guy with a wife and four kids who was willing to move out of the comfort zone of a secure job because he thought he could do better for his family, and for himself, by striking out on his own. I probably admire what he did more now than I did back then because as a father and family man myself I can understand the courage it took for him to face his fears and make that move. I understand now that he was under a great deal of pressure to support his family, but he faced his fears and succeeded. It took a lot of courage and perseverance. I know he was probably scared out of his mind that it wouldn't work, but he used that fear to create energy to get it done.

This wasn't an Olympic struggle or the sort of challenging situation you might read about in a magazine, but it was one of those quiet, brave struggles that people around the world go through every day. Life is never without challenges. Nor are there people who live without fear. The mark of courage is not ignoring fear; it is living with it and succeeding in spite of it.

Understanding Your Fears

The only effective way to overcome fears is to face them, to understand their origins and their impact on our lives, and to refuse to give in to them. I realized that when I accepted the invitation to speak at the stutterers' convention, but I have to admit it wasn't easy to get on that stage and face a ballroom packed with people who, like me, had been dealing with stuttering all their lives. True,

I had overcome my stutter, but I worried that it was contagious. It is always in the back of my mind that I have made a living as a public figure and that if my stutter ever came back full-force, I would be out of work. I have a great business with good people in the key positions, but it's not like I could step aside and appoint a new "Jake." I am responsible for the success of my company. I cannot run and hide from that responsibility, and so I cannot run or hide from my greatest fear. I face it every day, and I have learned to use that fear as a positive source of energy, focus, and drive.

The Trolls Under Our Beds

We each have our unique collection of fears. From childhood through adulthood, we build the collection, sometimes discarding old ones for new ones but generally maintaining a good representation of those that plague the human race in general: the fear of death, abandonment, loneliness, rejection, disapproval, and on and on.

As a child I had a unique fear—the fear of Bozo. I loved watching the show on television. But when my mom took me to the studio in New York, I freaked when I saw that orange hair and big nose. Bozophobia set in. I am still in recovery.

Every person has some way, good or bad, of dealing with fear. Some dull their fears with drink or drugs. Some hide from them by getting lost in soap operas or The Movie Channel. Some fight them off at aerobics or yoga class. Not all of these activities are bad or harmful, of course, but what *is* harmful is running from your fears.

If you are going to live your life to the fullest, to pursue your dreams and your Ultimate Goal, it is vital that you acknowledge your fears and learn how to overcome them so that you can live *fearlessly*. Living fearlessly doesn't necessarily mean that you live without fear. That may well be impossible, since fear is a very human and natural emotion. We have some very helpful fears such as the fear of falling, the fear of fire, the fear of hostile people with knives, and the fear of large carnivores with sharp teeth. To live fearlessly means to get past or beyond your fears by dealing with them as natural emotions.

The other night my daughter, Morgan, came to our room and woke up Tracey and me because she thought there was a troll under her bed. I didn't tell her to crawl in bed with us. Instead, I stood firm and announced in my best big strong "Dad" voice, "This is Morgan's daddy. If there are any trolls in here, they had better get out of this house right now!"

I walked the troll down the stairs and out of the house and I stood at the front door watching the troll leave. To this day, Morgan swears she heard that troll running down the stairs. She hasn't had the troll problem since. There will come a time when she will understand that trolls are not real, but I want her to understand that fear *is* a real emotion, and as an emotion, it can be dealt with.

The way to get beyond our fears is to examine our responses to them. What do children do when they become fearful? They get nervous and antsy. They can't sleep so they want to crawl into bed with you and snuggle into your confident, calm sleep. Either that or they try to get you to buy in to their nervousness by waking you up and telling you how frightened they are.

Adults like to tell stories about their children and the fears that drive them from their beds, but the truth is that most adults are driven by fear, too. Childhood fears of storms or monsters give way to adult fears of insecurity, being unloved, unsuccessful, or any number of other learned fears.

That's right, we teach ourselves to have these fears, often without giving much thought to their source. Many of our learned fears, in fact most of them, are rooted in emotions and beliefs that have little more basis in reality than the troll under the bed, but the fears themselves become real to us, and as a result, the *fear* becomes an obstacle in our lives.

The next time you feel an attack of fear coming on, make a note of the physical symptoms. Do you shake your legs, tap a pencil on the desk, drum your fingers, doodle on a writing pad? These are natural reactions to fear triggered deep in the brain. Fear creates energy, which, since we are not usually in fight-or-flight situations, we have to expend somehow. When you feel that nervous energy welling up, try to understand where it is coming from, what fear is triggering the physical response, and then calm yourself and get past it. For many people, fear triggers a sense of helplessness, but we rarely are helpless, and it is important to understand that.

How do you get past your fear? By understanding its origins, by acknowledging that some fears are quite natural, and by telling yourself that real courage involves not beating back or ignoring fear but using the abundant energy created by fear to acknowledge it, move past it, and go after what you want in spite of it!

I'm sure you know someone who was hurt in a bad relationship and developed a fear of committing to another relationship. That is an understandable fear, but also an unreasonable one and a hurtful one. You can't isolate yourself from love and companionship because of one failed relationship. Giving in to that fear may offer some protection, but it is not worth it to be lonely or never to experience the rewards of a loving and trusting relationship.

Like the troll under your childhood bed, your fears are as real as you make them. No matter how many times you tell yourself there are no such things as trolls, the image remains vivid. The more you tell yourself not to think about trolls, the more you do think about them. What do you fear most? Being alone? Being unsuccessful, or maybe being successful? Being insignificant? Being unloved? If you hold on to those fears without dealing with them, they only become more and more real to you.

You can have well-defined goals, a step-by-step plan to go after them, a lot of support and love, and all of the other essential elements for pursuing your Ultimate Goal, but if you are unwilling to acknowledge and face your fears, you will probably never achieve all that you dream of doing in your life.

Far too many people deny their fears, and some even choose to wallow in them: "I could never do that, I'm too afraid . . ." How many times have you heard that? Was it you saying it? If it was you, consider what the cost of that attitude might be. What if I had allowed my fear of stuttering again to keep me from starting a business or becoming an entertainer? What if we all decided to let our fear of that troll underneath the bed keep us from getting up and going on with our lives, or pursuing our Ultimate Goals?

A Pileup and a Meltdown

It was a major challenge for me to accept the invitation to speak at the stutterers' convention. When I first arrived at the event, in Anaheim, a young boy came up to me and asked for my autograph, and of course he stuttered badly. I used to hate it when people tried to help me while I stuttered. I wanted them to let me finish the thought. I knew the words, I was just stuck and I wanted to get through it as quickly as I could. So I tried to encourage him, but it was painful for me too, because I saw myself in that young boy. I revisited all of the pain that stuttering had brought me, and those memories gave more power to the fear that had been haunting me about making this appearance.

I confess that when I stood up to speak at that convention, I was more than a little nervous. Okay, I was terrified! The first words that came out of my mouth crashed into each other like a twenty-car pileup. I stumbled and stuttered and I was having such a hard time that finally I looked out to the audience and said, "Wow, this is contagious, guys!"

Everybody laughed!

That was all I needed. *They understood!*

All right, pop quiz time. What was I doing when I made the joke about stuttering being contagious? Time's up! I was using the nervous energy created by my fear of stuttering to get past that fear. When I channeled that energy into humor and the little joke, it brought laughter and carried me right past the fear. Was it their laughter that washed my fear away? I don't think so. It was their understanding of the process I was using. As stutterers, they had an abundant understanding of my fear. They saw that I was dealing with it and using the energy in a constructive manner—neither fighting nor fleeing, but riding it where *I* wanted to go.

That is the key. Nobody lives without fear—in fact, the most courageous people live openly *with* their fears. In acknowledging and using my fear to create positive energy, I won the fight that each of those stutterers wages every day, and they were happy for me. I didn't hide from fear or wallow in it, I simply got it out there where we all agreed it was not going to hold me back. The people in that audience understood, as you must, that the only way to grow is to face your fears every time they arise, acknowledge them, and direct that energy for your purposes.

I wish I could say that I come out on top every time when taking on my fears, but the truth is, sometimes a fear can catch you with your guard down. You may be tired, or ill, or just unprepared for the fight, and your fears will sneak up on you. It can happen. I know. It happened to me a few years ago when I was invited to appear on Al Roker's weekend morning show on NBC. I arrived at the studio in New York about two hours early and I was sitting in the greenroom by myself, feeling very relaxed, so relaxed that I might even have fallen asleep for a while. Then, suddenly, it was time to go on, and a producer came and got me and escorted me out onto this tiny set with everybody running around in a tizzy. This was a live show, which tends to make everyone a little edgy anyway, and I went from being very relaxed to suddenly being uptight with all the frenzy around me.

Enter Mr. Fear. It really caught me off guard. When the interview started, I underwent a complete mental meltdown. I couldn't get out the words that I had planned to say. The connection between my brain and my vocal cords seemed to be jammed. I stumbled over words, speaking what seemed like gibberish to me. Suddenly, I was back in ninth grade, humiliated in front of the class.

My five minutes with Al Roker seemed like five days. I left the studio like a man fleeing prison. I returned to the hotel and told Tracey, "I blew it." She had watched the show and she told me it wasn't that bad, although I had seemed unusually nervous. I was upset with myself for a few hours because in a weak moment I had psyched myself into letting my fear overcome me instead of using that nervous energy as I had at the stutterers' convention.

Tracey said it seemed worse to me because I am so self-conscious about it, and she is probably right. She also reminded me that this was one of the very few times that I'd lost the battle. When you consciously face your fears, you will win the vast majority of the time, but there may be times when your fears sneak up on you and momentarily shake your confidence.

At those times, reflect on your victories, not the losses. Build strength on the positive experiences you have had. In the end, the most important thing is to face your fears rather than hiding from them, because you can't live your life in hiding. Even if you don't always win, you can draw confidence from the fact that you have the courage to face your fears.

The Fear Face-off

When you set out to pursue your Ultimate Goal, you are going to experience fears. Here are ways to deal with those fears:

1. *Identify the fear.*

   What *exactly* is this fear? Is it a fear of failure or a fear of success? Are you afraid what other people will say or think about you if you fail? Or are you afraid that you won't be able to handle success? Work at identifying your fear and then give it a name so that you can deal with it as something that has a negative impact on your life and determine that you are going to handle it. You can handle it. You may have one fear or nine hiding under the bed and dogging your life, but if you summon the courage to identify each of them, then you are on the way to understanding and conquering them.

2. *Take that fear on.*

   Don't make the mistake of trying to run from it or work around it, under it, or over it. Take it head on. Get under the bed and look that troll in the eyes. If I had not accepted the speaking engagement, I would have missed an opportunity to successfully confront my fear, and those victories are like money in the bank. When I had the meltdown on the Roker show, I might have felt like I could never do another appearance if I hadn't successfully faced the far greater challenge of talking to a large group of stutterers. With that successful speech in the bank, I was able to better handle the meltdown and explain it as being more related to my weariness than an inability to speak clearly. In fact, when we launched *Body by Jake* magazine, I appeared on the *Today* show with Al Roker, and it was a grand slam.

3. *Tap into your fear and use that energy.*

When you feel a fear taking hold of you, teach yourself to look for the energy outlet. Are you fidgeting or talking too much, or is it venting through the emotions of anger and anxiety? It is impossible to sit quietly and calmly when fear is present, so there must be some expression. Your job is to redirect that energy into a positive action appropriate to your goals. This is when you reach into your heart for the courage to turn your fear into fuel. Martial arts experts talk about turning negative energy into a positive force. In judo, you are trained to use your opponent's power against him. When he pushes, you redirect that energy so that your opponent suffers the negative consequences, not you.

When you feel fear coming on, welcome it as a natural and instinctive emotion preparing you to face a challenge and then direct all of the energy it creates to a positive purpose that moves you forward. In an early episode in the first season of *Big Brother Jake,* my original sitcom on the Family Channel, I ran into a mental block when it came to a certain line in the sixty-page script. I don't know why, but this one line just wouldn't stick in my head, so I wrote it on my hand. We did that show live in front of an audience, so there was no way to just stop and redo it when the time came. I was really nervous as we started doing the show. I grew more and more nervous as we got closer to the troublesome line.

Just before it came time for my line, I waited until I was off camera and I glanced down at my hand to give myself one last reminder. But I was so nervous, I had sweated the ink off my hand. Everybody stopped and looked at me, thinking either I was going to run off stage or my head was going to explode. Instead, I used all that nervous energy and blurted out, "I forgot the line. It was on my hand and I sweated it off!" Obviously, we couldn't keep that in the show, but it got a big laugh and we taped over it later so that it worked fine on television.

Now, admittedly, that was not a great victory over fear, but it also wasn't a surrender. I didn't run and hide or give up. I hung in there, and sometimes just staying in the fight and facing your fears is a victory. Everyone has fears. Everybody has to deal with them. You are not alone in this. Put that in the bank, and understand that anytime you can transfer the negative energy of fear into positive action, you are winning the battle.

Improvising Fearlessness

Although I've had a fear of stuttering since childhood, I've also had a rather incompatible dream of being a stand-up comedian. I was always the class clown in school. I used humor to win acceptance and to overcome my insecurity about my stutter. My chance to realize that dream of being a comedian came while I was renewing the Body by Jake television series, which was going into its second season in syndication. It was the 1989 annual convention of the National Association of Producers and Television Executives (NAPTE) in Houston. Budd Friedman, creator of the *Evening at the Improv* comedy show, stopped by my booth to say hello, and during our conversation I told him that I'd always wanted to host his show. I didn't tell him I wanted to do stand-up on it, because as much as I had dreamed of doing that, I was not sure I was ready for it. I knew you also needed material, and although I had a lot of stories to tell, I had never tested them on a big audience.

Budd said he would like to have me do his show, but at the time I thought he was just being polite. But the next week, he called. Do you know the old saying "Be careful what you wish for because you might get it"? I was excited about doing his show, but nervous, too. Especially when I found out that the host didn't just read jokes off a TelePrompTer and introduce guests. I was expected to have a stand-up routine.

"You are going to need four minutes of material," the producer said. "The host does a four-minute routine. You know, giggles, chuckles, belly-shaking, tears running down the cheeks, side-aching laughs?"

Material? I didn't have "material." I had stories about my life that I thought were funny, but I didn't have material. That sounded so . . . so materialistic. When I told the producer I didn't have any formal, professionally done material, he had the show's writers work up some stuff, but I didn't like it. They were jokes about being a personal fitness trainer and I thought they were too canned and pretty corny. They weren't the stories that I was comfortable telling, like about my bar mitzvah, or funny weight-training stories that had always made my relatives laugh.

The day after being invited to host *An Evening at the Improv*, I went home and told Tracey and she was pretty excited for me because she knew this was a dream of mine. She wasn't so excited when I told her I didn't want her to be there.

"Look, honey, I'm really, really nervous about this. I'm flashing back to the old grade-school days when I'd nearly get sick at the thought of giving a book report because of my stutter. I feel like I'm probably going to go down in flames at the Improv, and I don't think I want you to see it."

Tracey wasn't buying that. "You've always said we're a team. I want to be there to support you," she said.

"When we're winning, we are a team, but when I'm losing, I don't want to take you down with me," I said.

I know it was weak. But at that point, we had been married only a few months. I didn't want my new wife to see me go down in a ball of flames.

Think about it. Most comedians trying out a new act go to some low-profile club in Keokuk or Poughkeepsie. They don't put their neck on the block in L.A., in front of a national television audience.

The night came, and I got there early. From backstage, I peeked out through the curtain and watched people filing in. They looked hip, sophisticated, tough. *Definitely* a tough crowd. I was sweating like I'd just had a three-hour workout. It didn't help when Garry Shandling, one of the top comedians in the universe, walked up to me backstage and said, "You look pretty nervous, Jake."

"I am, Garry."

"Don't worry, buddy. You're gonna bomb."

He laughed. I didn't.

It was time to go on. I stepped out into the spotlights. I took the microphone in hand, gulped, and took a deep breath.

They laughed.

I told a story about being the world's only Jewish bodybuilder.

They laughed.

I told a bar mitzvah story.

They laughed.

I told them that bodybuilders never breathe and always wear extra-small T-shirts.

They laughed.

The red light came on, indicating it was time for the host to introduce the night's first comic.

I ignored it and told another story.

Their bellies were shaking. Their ribs were aching. Tears were running down their cheeks. I think they are *still* laughing.

I was a huge hit, if I must say so myself.

POWERLIVING
LESSON NO. 9

Be Like Womba

One of the first celebrities I got to know personally when I moved to Los Angeles was Tommy Chong of the comedy team Cheech and Chong. Tommy and I worked out at the same gym and we got to know each other there. Although Tommy was a professional comedian with a vast following for his comedy albums and a big hit movie, *Up in Smoke,* I did most of the entertaining during our workouts. I told him stories of my crazy experiences as the Hulk at the Universal Studios Tour.

There was plenty of comedy material in that job. In the show, people in the audience were brought on stage to be made up by a professional makeup team. I was the comic relief. While they were being made up, I'd jump out from backstage as the Hulk and scare the face paint right off them.

It may not have been an acting role worthy of an Academy Award nomination, but it paid the rent on my $199-a-month Studio City apartment. Sometimes people who were serious fans of the Hulk came on the tour thinking I really was Lou Ferrigno, the actor who played the role in the television series. If they were real fans, they knew that Lou had a hearing impairment, so they'd come up to me during the autograph session and yell in my ear, "HOW YA DOIN', LOUIE???"

Being mistaken for Lou and being screamed at were two of the more enjoyable aspects of this job. Tommy Chong thought I had the craziest job he'd ever heard of, and he particularly enjoyed the fact that whenever I got up from using a workout bench at the gym I'd leave a little green behind. One day after we'd been trading stories, he asked me if I had a SAG card. I told him nothing on me sagged, I'd been working out for years.

"What's a SAG card?"

He explained that it was proof of membership in the Screen Actors Guild, and you had to have it in order to be in the movies. Then he offered me my first acting job. "We're writing a sequel to *Up in Smoke* and maybe we could create a role for you in it based on your Hulk stories," he said. "Come to my house tomorrow night and meet my wife and Cheech and tell them some of these stories and we'll come up with something for you."

Going Hollywood

As it turned out, I was invited back to Tommy's house in Bel Air four or five times over the next few weeks as he and Cheech Marin worked on the sequel, which they had ingeniously titled *Cheech and Chong's Next Movie*. Although they had cultivated an image as a couple of wild and crazy, pot-smoking guys, in truth they were hard workers and very sharp businessmen along with being extremely funny. They wrote a part for me in their movie based on the Hulk on the Universal Studios Tour, but they changed the name—and the skin tone—so as not to get in a trademark battle with the people who owned the real Hulk name.

When Tommy brought a script to the gym for me to read, I couldn't believe it. They wanted me to play Womba, a bumbling red superhero in their movie. It was a costarring role and a really big part for a guy who'd never been on a movie set. Along with being big and red, Womba was a bull-in-the-china-shop kind of superhero. He was always walking through the wrong walls and trying to rescue the wrong people. It was a great part and I was really excited about it.

The day after they showed me the script, Tommy and his producer, Howard Brown, met with me and my parents, who had moved to Tarzana, near L.A. "Mr. and Mrs. Steinfeld, your son Jake is going to be a big star, so be prepared. This is going to be a very big movie," Brown said.

I called all my friends back on Long Island and told them that a star was being born even before we started filming. I was getting paid a couple grand a week to be in a movie! I even had my own little trailer on the set, and all the free food I could eat, which was a lot. I was having a ball.

Everything went great until I was getting ready to leave my apartment to go to the set for the third day of shooting my scenes. That morning, I got a telephone call from the line producer, Peter McGregor Scott.

"Jake, mate," said Peter, "I have some good news and some bad news. We have been looking at the dailies and the executives at the studio think your work is fantastic, but they have a problem. They say that a two-hundred-forty-five-pound guy painted red dominates every scene in the movie and they aren't paying to have a two-hundred-forty-five-pound red guy be the star, they are paying for Cheech and Chong."

This did not sound good for Womba.

"I'll stand behind some plants or something," I offered, but I knew what was coming next.

"Jake, I'm sorry, but they've told me to cut Womba from the movie," Peter said. "The good news is that we will leave you in one scene and you will still be given your full pay. Oh, and you can keep eating with us if you want, too."

I felt like Hollywood had opened the door and invited me in, and then slammed that same door in my face. I was devastated.

I told everybody in the world that I was going to be a star in a Cheech and Chong movie. All my friends back home. All the guys in the gym. I won't be able to walk out of this apartment. I'm finished in show business.

I think I sat in my apartment for a while talking to the potted plant, which wasn't very sympathetic. I was nineteen years old and my Hollywood career was already over. Womba was washed up.

Success Is Failure Turned Inside Out

Tommy and Cheech called me and said they were sorry, but that I shouldn't take it so hard. "Things are going to be great for you out here," they said. "We've all been through this sort of thing, it's part of the business."

It was tough for me to see that then, just as it is difficult for anyone going through hard times to focus on the positive rather than the negative aspects of failure. For a short time, I made the mistake that many people make. I focused on the door that had been closed on me, instead of looking for doors that were opening up.

How many times have you done that? We all do it from time to time. Some people do it *all* the time. We look at failure as final, instead of understanding that when one door closes, another opens up. It was shortly after Womba died on the cutting-room floor that I created my own business and I became a celebrity by an entirely different route. The funny thing is that when I told my clients about my experience as Womba, each and every one of them had their own version of it. They had all been rejected for big roles or cut out of movies early in their careers. They'd been told they had the wrong look, the wrong build, a bad nose, a weird voice, or not enough talent for the role.

In talking to them, I realized that the biggest stars in Hollywood are *lifelong failures.* From my conversations with the wealthiest and most dynamic businesspeople and entrepreneurs that I've known, I can say that nearly all of them are lifelong failures, too. That is, most of them have been experiencing and going through *failures* to get to their *successes* all of their lives.

I too aspire to be a lifelong failure, because when you fail at something, it means you are striving and pushing the envelope. Failure is an indicator that you are fighting for success. Many of the most successful people in the world are lifelong failures. Ted Turner fails. Warren Buffett fails. Michael Jordan fails. Nelson Mandela fails.

Do their failures stop them from being successful? No, in fact, their failures are critical to their successes. Whether they measure their success in terms of money in the bank, points on the scoreboard, or good deeds accomplished, truly successful people understand that when you are chasing dreams and goals, failure is part of the process. They all fail because they are striving for goals. They are chasing their dreams. But they do not view failure as the end of the process, merely a part of the process.

The only way to never experience failure is to never go after anything worth succeeding at. Failure is a growing pain. It is the ache in a muscle that is sore because it is being stretched and strengthened. Do you know what bodybuilders do to build muscle? They *go for failure*. That means they lift weights until their muscles are exhausted and they fail to lift the weight anymore. They push themselves to the absolute limit, so that they can see where the limits are and determine where it is they want to go next. They know that by breaking down the old muscle tissue, they can then build even greater strength. *Going for failure* is part of their process for building success.

Failure Will Find You, and Help You

Failure will find you, whether you welcome it or not. You cannot hide from it. The key is to accept it and use it to your advantage. Failure helps you set the limits of where you are, so that you can see where it is you want to go. Every success you attain will at some point look like a sure failure. Failing is not the challenge. Failing doesn't keep you from succeeding. Only *you* can do that by deciding that failure is a permanent state instead of a temporary condition, a stepping-stone to your goal—which itself is merely one stage of the continuous upward spiral of PowerLiving.

Here is a challenge for you. Before you finish reading this chapter, get in touch with the most successful person you know. Ask that person if he or she has ever failed at something. I absolutely guarantee that the person will immediately call to mind a failure that at the time made them feel as though they would never, ever be successful.

What does that tell you? It should tell you what every scientist, businessperson, and athlete embraces: Failure is nothing to be feared or to feel defeated about. Failure is part of the process of success.

The businessman knows that not every deal is going to work. The athlete absolutely knows that a high percentage of his or her shots, swings, leaps, or throws will fall short of the mark. The inventor knows that part of the scientific process involves working through failures until he finds the formula that does the job. The genetic engineers who cloned Dolly—the sheep, not Parton—spent years and years learning from their hundreds of failures before they found success. We all need to understand, as they do, that success is failure turned inside out.

Failure Is Not Dying, It Is Living

Why do so many people have such a difficult time with failure, then? Intellectually, we know that most of the time life will go on for us, unless our failure involves a malfunctioning parachute at 30,000 feet. The problem is that so many believe that failure is a permanent condition. They are conditioned to living out of their current circumstances. They do not use or trust their imagination to light the way. They see failure as their inescapable destiny, which would be downright silly if it weren't so sad. Snap out of it!

When Womba went down on the cutting-room floor, I was only nineteen years old. I had been living in L.A. only a few months. I had already met and become friends with two of the hottest stars in town, Cheech and Chong, and I had worked on a movie set with them. Was I a failure because my character proved to be so dominant that it was cut from the movie? No, not at all. Had I failed? No.

So who made me a failure? Womba made me do it. *I* took the failure personally. *I* let it make me insecure. *I* sentenced myself to solitary confinement with the potted plant. The failure wasn't the problem. It is only natural to feel disappointment when things don't work out the way you had hoped, but there is no reason to feel *defeated*. We are never defeated unless we quit!

I know of a successful Hollywood executive, one of the wealthiest men in the entertainment business; he has a great family and a huge circle of friends, but when just one of his television shows was canceled, he took it as a defeat. But he chose to focus on this one defeat rather than to live out of his successes.

When this series was canceled, he went into a depression and then he literally went to bed and refused to leave the bedroom for an entire year. He personalized the failure of that one television series. He should have known better. You should know better, too. Have you ever heard someone say, "I'll die if I don't get this job"? Or "If this doesn't work out I'll just die"? What is that person doing? Associating failure with death. Failure is not death, is it? Each of us experiences some sort of failure every day, yet life goes on.

Failure has nothing to do with death. In fact, it has everything to do with life and with growth. Those who try and fail are going after life. They are chasing their dreams and their Ultimate Goals. That is PowerLiving!

Focus on Success Even in Failure

A few years after Womba went down, I had another acting opportunity, this time for a summer replacement television show on ABC called *Shaping Up* with the king of deadpan comedy, Leslie Nielsen. Originally I was asked to come on for just one show, but my appearance went over so well that they signed me on for all six episodes. The show was set in a health club and I was cast as an airline attendant bodybuilder—a strange mix, you have to admit, but that is comedy. I had a great time. It was my first sitcom. It was in front of a live audience. The immediate laughter was great, and I had some wonderful lines. I worked hard on the show to make the character funny and interesting, and I got great feedback from people I trust.

After the first episode, they did a special screening of the show for the press, and the reaction at the screening appeared to be great. I went to it, and the people told me they thought I was hysterical. Once again, I got myself all psyched up. The day after the press screening, I went for breakfast to my favorite deli in Beverly Hills and there I picked up the latest edition of *The Holly-*

wood Reporter, which is the entertainment industry bible. I found a review of the show there and I sat down with my egg whites and large orange juice, ready to read about how wonderful I was.

I didn't read that. What I read was a review calling me "the gym dumbbell" and the show "*terrible.*"

Nice line. When I read that, it cut like a rope around my neck. Remember the concept of always building and protecting your brand value? I take that concept very seriously. I regarded that critic's cheap shot as a blow not only to my brand value, but also to my budding career as an actor. At this point, my business as a fitness motivator was really booming and I was hoping to spin my acting career from that success. This review seemed to send me spinning the wrong way.

I carried a heavy load on my rounds that day. But at every stop and with every star, I got the same response. I asked Jennifer Jones and Steven Spielberg and Bette Midler if they'd ever gotten a bad review.

"You think THAT'S a bad review? Let me show you some of mine!"

Harrison Ford, in particular, was unsympathetic. As I've mentioned before, Harrison is a regular guy. He has had to work hard for his success and he took a lot of knocks along the way. Some critics even ripped *Star Wars* in the early days, before it became one of the most successful movies of all time. When I told him about the "dumbbell" review, he laughed out loud.

"Thanks, pal," I said.

"Look," he responded, "if you are going to believe the good reviews, you have to believe the bad ones too. At least they're writing about you. At least you're getting roles. Think of all the people out there waiting tables and working as carpenters who dream of just having a shot at it."

I think they miscast Harrison in *Star Wars.* Instead of Han Solo, he should have been Yoda, the wise Jedi master. He and all of my other clients reminded me that I was already successful as an actor in many ways, and that the secret was to build on my success rather than focusing on failure, because the things that you focus on become your reality.

I have a friend who attended one of those race-car driver's schools and they had a session on what to do when your car is spinning toward the retaining wall on the track. The instructor told him that the biggest mistake drivers make when their car goes into a spin is to look at the wall, because people unconsciously tend to steer where they are looking. Over and over they practiced looking away from the wall in order to regain control and to steer away from disaster. The wall represents failure, and if you focus on failure, you will fail. But if you look away from failure, you can focus instead on doing what you need to do to steer toward success.

Don't Let Failure Jinx You

Shortly after I received the "dumbbell" review, I was offered a leading-man role as the costar of another television pilot, and I got it. Luckily, I hadn't gone into a deep depression over the one bad review and jumped off a bridge. It seems silly when you look at it that way, doesn't it?

Bette Midler was another of my celebrity clients who told me to get over the bad review and to focus on success instead. When I began training her, Bette had just come off some bad reviews herself for the 1981 movie *Jinxed*. Two years earlier, she had been nominated for an Academy Award for her performance in *The Rose*. But Bette was back and not about to give up or go into hiding. "Jake, baby, it can only get better, because it can't get any worse," she said.

Like me, as a kid Bette had her share of challenges. But Bette believes in herself, and she is one very determined lady. What I really remember about our early days working together was that the telephone at her house rarely rang. If you've been around many big stars, particularly those who are on a roll, you learn quickly that the telephone rings around the clock with calls from talent agents and publicists, investment advisers, and entertainment reporters.

In 1985, Bette landed a leading role in a new movie with Nick Nolte and Richard Dreyfuss, *Down and Out in Beverly Hills*. People always laugh when they see someone else fall, but it is a nervous laugh because they feel it could happen to them too. As it turned out, in this case the joke was on the critics. That movie was a major hit and it resurrected the careers of all three stars. It is now a Hollywood legend how Bette, Nick, and Richard all rose to become major players once again because of that movie. I was working with Bette when *Down and Out* became a hit, and I can attest to what it did for her career. After it was released, the phone rang constantly at Bette's house, and we could hardly get a workout in because of all of the studio executives who came calling. They were tripping over Barbara Walters and others now eager to do a story on the rebirth of a star. Failure had not killed Bette Midler's career because Bette had refused to let that happen, just as countless other highly successful people have weathered failures by focusing instead on success.

Do you know that when George Lucas previewed his first *Star Wars* movie for his friends, most were afraid it would be a failure at the box office? What if George had tossed his "failed" movie in the trash basket? What if Michael Jordan had given up on basketball after he was cut from the team in junior high? What if Ted Turner had listened to all those people who laughed at his concept of a twenty-four-hour news channel and said that CNN must stand for Chicken Noodle News?

Fortunately, I didn't give up on my acting career when Womba was cut from most of my first movie, or when I got that bad review. Obviously, it's a good thing I didn't take my early failures seriously, because nobody else did. My opportunities today are greater than ever before.

The Fear of Not Failing

It seems to me that the only people who allow failure to defeat them are those who fear *success*. It's true that success can be scary for people who haven't prepared themselves for it. Hollywood is full of stories about actors, directors, and studio executives who have attained incredible success and then self-destructed on drugs, or alcohol, or by some other method. Very often, this self-destruction is triggered not by a fear of failure but by a fear of success. Either consciously or unconsciously, such people may feel undeserving or unable to maintain the level of success.

What is the remedy for this fear of success? You have to build the framework before you put the roof on the house. You have to have the infrastructure, the imagination, the support network of Go-To People, and a relentless commitment to dreams and goals. Those who have experienced failure along the way to success have often been strengthened in the way that a flame forges and strengthens steel.

So what do you do when you experience a failure or a setback? Going to your room for a year and crying is one option, but it's not a very attractive one, unless you have one heck of a bedroom. Here are a few useful methods for successfully dealing with a failure.

1. *Step back from it and put it in perspective.*

   Even small setbacks can seem overwhelming if you live within them. If you've failed at something at work or in your relationship, it is wise to take a break of some kind, whether it is a few days away from the office or some time away from the friend or loved one. It's impossible to get a good perspective when you are still wrapped up in the emotions of the situation. Get out of the hothouse environment to a place where you can breathe comfortably. For some, this may mean retreating to a quiet place to be alone. For others, it may mean joining a lively and supportive group of friends, or maybe just one person who is sympathetic and who brings out the best in you. Turn the heat down, so that you can think through the failure and see your way past it.

2. *Call a meeting.*

   Once you have escaped the overheated emotional state that failure sometimes creates, take time to recap what happened. Look at it as though you were an outsider trying to understand it. Look at it from every angle. Once you have become more objective about it, discuss what happened with someone whose judgment you trust.

3. *Decide what is not working.*

I realized that becoming a competitive bodybuilder was not going to work for me because I was not willing to take steroids. Did I fail in going after that dream? No, I believe the dream failed me. It didn't work for me, so I set out in search of new peaks to climb. Don't give up when failure knocks you down. Back off. Decide what isn't working. And then decide what will work. Get back into the battle with new equipment and a new plan of attack.

4. *Pull out your best weapon against failure, your sense of humor.*

"You are going to laugh about this someday." I don't know how old that saying is, but I do know how *true* it is. The people who tend to view failure as a finality are most often the same people who say things like "It's never going to stop raining" or "I can't possibly get all of this work done." These are people with very limited vision, and if they don't expand their vision, they will lead very limited lives. I don't know about you, but when I find the humor in a situation, it expands my vision. Humor requires that you step back and see things in perspective, and that gives you a wider view. Laughter also causes chemical reactions within the body that flood your system with soothing and calming sensations.

When failure has you in its grip, grab a good comedy, a funny book, or a friend who makes you laugh and tap into nature's gift of laughter. Failure is no match for good humor.

America's Funniest Failures

If they ever have an awards show for comic failures, I will gladly volunteer to be the host. I can see the promo spots now, *"America's Funniest Failures,* starring Jake Steinfeld, creator of the infamous AerobiStick."

Take the AerobiStick. Please.

The AerobiStick was one of the dumbest ideas that we ever loved at Body by Jake Enterprises. It was an early product we tried to develop and market. The concept grew out of the fact that I had been training my celebrity clients with basic household items like broomsticks, so we wanted to develop a product like that. The challenge was, we got away from the keep-it-simple concept and after a while we were looking at sticks filled with colored water, sticks with rubber tips, sticks that played the theme from *Rocky,* you name it.

Eventually, we ended up with the AerobiStick, and I am too proud to tell you how many of them we *still* have in a warehouse somewhere in this country. The AerobiStick was not one of our great success stories, but it was one of our funniest failures.

Another Idea That Didn't Wash

Part of being an entrepreneur, of course, is always looking for fresh business opportunities. Every successful entrepreneur has been unsuccessful. Many have been bankrupt and wiped out several times, but often they come back big because they learn from their mistakes and failures and keep pushing on. But then, sometimes they have even funnier failures, such as Body by Jake Shampoo.

A manufacturer of skin- and hair-care products from New York contacted us shortly after we opened our fitness studio in Manhattan and wanted to make a licensing deal with us for shampoo and other products. We told the manufacturer to send us some samples of the shampoo. When the samples came, I gave some to my lawyer, Bob Lieberman, and to Phil Scotti, the president of Body by Jake.

I tried my sample of Body by Jake Shampoo the next morning when I showered. About twenty minutes later, my head started itching real bad. By the time I got to the office there were phone messages from both Bob and Phil. They had tried the shampoo, too, and they were both scratching like a couple of flea-bitten mutts. In fact, all three of us considered shaving our heads, our skin itched so badly. We decided that the only way we would lend my brand name to that product was if it was to be sold as a prank product, like itching powder. Then we'd call it Itching by Jake.

See? I've learned to laugh at failure. Now if you will just fill out the form at the back of the book and send in fifty dollars, I'll gladly send you a case of this hilarious mistake.

See, I've failed and I've survived. In fact, I've failed and I've thrived. You will fail too. Understand that it is *going to happen.* Be prepared for it, and then look for the doors that are opening up for you!

POWERLIVING
LESSON NO. 10

Make a Change and Make It Work

The very first job I landed when I moved from Long Island to Los Angeles was in Vince's, a small bodybuilding gym in Studio City. It was located near many of the big television and movie studios, so a lot of the stars would come in to work out. I was nineteen years old and really psyched about being in Hollywood. I could hardly sleep, I was so charged up about making a positive change in my life.

When you make a change in order to go after your dreams and goals, you will run a gauntlet of emotions both positive and negative. One of the positive things is that your senses become finely tuned. You notice everything around you. Have you ever gone through a breakup with someone you really cared about, and then, during that transitional period that followed, you found that every song you hear on the radio is about breaking up, or love, or loneliness? That's because when you go through a change, your senses are heightened. Your antennae are fully extended and you are emotionally charged. You see and smell and feel things with a higher degree of sensitivity. Both times after Morgan and Nicky were born and safely home, I can remember thinking the sky looked bluer and the grass greener and the air felt crisper. Change was in the air, and it was flowing through me, too.

Your senses and emotions are heightened during periods of change, whether that change is brought about by events that happen *to* you or that you bring about yourself. Why is it that so many people remember where they were when they learned that President John F. Kennedy had been assassinated? Because his assassination disrupted the flow of everyday life and triggered a significant period of change. An entire nation was thrown into a period of mourning and a heightened emotional state. As you grow older, most of the events that stand out in your memory are those that occurred during periods of change, because the emotions you felt during those times were so intense that they have been implanted in your memory.

I'll never forget my first few weeks in California. L.A. was a whole new world for me, a different climate, a different attitude. Everything looked and smelled different. One of the things that I really got a kick out of in those early California days was seeing celebrities come into Vince's to work out. I worked behind the reception desk and I think it was my first or second day on the job when in walked the costar of one of my favorite television shows, Kent McCord of *Adam-12*. Being a fan, I did the really cool thing and immediately let fly with my imitation of a police radio dispatcher calling for "One Adam-Twelve, One Adam-Twelve. See the lady on Fourth Street, family disturbance."

Not surprisingly, McCord looked at me like I was a complete chucklehead.

A short time later, along came another of my Hollywood favorites, Carl Weathers, who played Apollo Creed in the *Rocky* movies. Naturally, I did my a cappella version of the "Theme from Rocky." Weathers glared at me like I was some vile alien life form. To tell you the truth, once the initial rush of making the move to California began to wear off, I did feel like an intruder from another planet. Earlier, I mentioned that during periods of change, most people experience a heightened emotional state that includes both good and bad sensations. I went through the positive fairly quickly, it seemed, and then sank down into the negative.

I had made the move because I had been wasting my time and my parents' money in college. My folks and I both realized that. It took some hard selling and I am sure my parents thought my goal was frivolous, but they eventually agreed that if becoming Mr. America was my dream, I should go after it. I am sure that it was difficult for them, but they supported my decision. They even gave me $3,000 and leased me a 1977 Camaro. They told me that if I failed I could come back home to them. There were more than a few times when I very nearly took them up on that offer.

There I was in La-La Land handing out towels to the stars, but I wasn't connecting with them or with anything else. It was like I was watching a movie that everybody else was starring in. At home and at college, I had been a star in my own universe. I was a body-builder, an athlete, and a leader in my own little circle. In L.A., I was just another muscular kid scraping to get by. I'd go home from work to my cramped apartment with only a black-and-white portable TV and my potted palm to keep me company. One of the loneliest things I think I ever did was watch the 1978 World Series between the Dodgers and the Yankees by myself in that apartment. Nobody to cheer with, nobody to argue with. I was a lonely guy.

Never before had I had a problem making friends, but I didn't fit in easily with the slick Hollywood crowd. I felt like a Wolverine boot on the Gucci rack. I was Long Island loud and gregarious; everybody else was California cool. I was so discombobulated that one night, when a really nice-looking gal came to my door and asked if I had any sugar, I thought she really was looking for sugar. I said no, and she left. I didn't get it. I wasn't getting anything, or anywhere. Even my potted plant was starting to wilt around the edges.

I had left college and my friends and family, and a longtime girl-friend, too, in order to change my life for the better. I had finally identified some goals for myself and decided to make things happen by making this change. But it was tougher than I thought it would be. It was the farthest I had ever been from home and it was also the first time I had had to deal with real loneliness and isolation and all of the other emotions involved in making a big move.

It was a time of great change in my life, and while change is often a method for improving your life, it can be intimidating and emotionally challenging. Change is tough. It can be nasty. It can get you alone in a dark room and bang away on you. I was determined to chase my dream, but I wasn't prepared for all the emotions that accompanied the changes I'd made in my life. I didn't know then what I know now: that there is a process for dealing with change. In this chapter I am going to teach that process to you.

When you really want to make things happen in your life and to grow as an individual, whether mentally, spiritually, or physically, you have to enact some sort of change. If you aren't happy with what you have been getting out of life, you have to change what you have been doing. It is as simple as that.

The Process of Change

Change is an integral part of all of our lives. It is a necessary and natural process that we all go through, and just as there is a pattern to the changes of the seasons in nature, there is a pattern of emotions that accompanies change in your life. Without a doubt, managing your emotions and actions during times of change is challenging, but it can be helpful if you *understand* the process of change so that you are prepared for all that comes with it.

If you go into it knowing that you are going to experience a wide range of emotions and feelings, and that those reactions are natural, then you can prepare yourself and deal with change rather than being overwhelmed by it. We really cannot manage change any more than we can control the seasons. But we can control how we *respond* to the things that happen to us, including the changes that occur in our lives. It is within our power to determine whether we accept and deal positively with the emotions and events that accompany a period of change, or whether we let the negative aspects drag us down, hold us back, or scare us into running back into that comfort zone.

In order to chase your dreams and to continually grow as a person throughout your lifetime, you will undoubtedly have to go through some difficult changes. Whether you are changing jobs or careers, making a change in a relationship, or moving to a new town, you will have to abandon your comfort zone, and that can give rise to all sorts of fears and emotions. There will be times in your life, too, when you have to deal with changes that you have no control over, such as the death of a loved one, or being downsized or transferred from your job. The key to coping with change in your life is to anticipate that there will be some rocky times during the transition. Understand that feelings of loneliness, isolation, self-doubt, and even discombobulation are to be expected when you leave your comfort zone.

You have to learn to think of life as an adventure and to understand that with every adventure there will be unexpected twists and turns, peaks and valleys, that make it challenging and fulfilling.

The first stage in the process of change that you create in your own life is the one I underwent when I found myself standing in my skimpy Cortland State lacrosse uniform in the freezing cold at Syracuse. That was what I call:

Stage 1: The Hammer over the Head

This is the point at which it dawns on you that you must seize control of your own life and make a change. This revelation is sometimes brought on by getting hit over the head with a hammer. In my case, it was a fairly light tap to the skull: My grades stank, I was taking courses I didn't care about, and my life wasn't moving *toward* anything. In other cases, the hammer may come down harder. You may get fired from your job because you aren't committed to doing what it takes. Your relationship falls apart. You wake up one day and realize that you aren't anywhere near where you want to be.

The truth is, most people know long before the hammer hits that they should make a change, but they are afraid to do what is necessary. Often, even when our circumstances are unhealthy or unsatisfying, we cling to the familiar because it is less scary than the great unknown that we will encounter if we make a change. That is why so many people stay in jobs they don't like or remain involved in unhealthy relationships. Eventually, though, the hammer comes down. Something happens that forces you to admit that you have to make a change. Your partner throws you out or leaves. Your boss fires or demotes you or cuts your pay. Something hits you over the head, and finally, the great motivator, *pain,* makes an appearance. Most of the changes we make in life come down to the simple fact that it is human nature to move away from pain and toward pleasure. If it becomes too painful to keep on doing what we have been doing, then, like the old dog sleeping under the hot porch, we will finally get up and look for someplace more comfortable.

When the hammer falls, it forces us to evaluate our current position in relation to our long-term vision: Am I where I should be? Where am I headed? Is this job a dead end or am I in position to get where I want to go? Is this relationship strong enough to hold up? Do I want it to hold up? Does this person bring out the best in me? Are we good for each other?

Once you are forced into asking those critical questions, you also begin asking what your options and alternatives are: What do I need to do to regain control over my life? How can I get back on track to what I really want? What do I need to do to get out of this dead-end job? this hurtful relationship? these painful circumstances?

If you identify alternatives and options that are more appealing because they offer more pleasure than pain, then you will be motivated to make a change, and that takes us to the second stage of the process of change:

Stage 2: The Breakaway

It's a basic truth that in order to move on to where you want to go, you have to leave someplace or something behind. Breaking away from your past and current circumstances can be both exciting and scary. As in any trip you take, there is the thrill of anticipation, along with the uncertainty and foreboding of what you may run into.

When you move from a house you have lived in for a long time to a new house, you may be excited about living in a better place, but that move is also accompanied by fears and concerns about packing and protecting all of your belongings, about leaving old neighbors behind, about whether the new house is affordable and right for you and your family.

These are all natural concerns, although sometimes people become confused as to why they feel depressed while packing for a move that they had undertaken in order to improve the quality of their living quarters. The same holds true for people who make the move to improve the quality of their lives. They decide to make the move because they are looking forward, which is good, but in doing that they sometimes neglect to make the break with what they are leaving behind, and then, later, they are surprised to feel saddened and remorseful.

This is related to the process of grieving, the emotional state that you go through when you lose a loved one or go through some other traumatic experience. There are a lot of theories on how to handle grief, but one thing that most experts agree on is that you can't *cheat* your grief. You have to express it, and it is better to express it sooner than later.

I know a guy who grew up in a violent neighborhood riddled with gangs and guns. Two of his older brothers had been gang members and both of them died in gang violence. This guy had seen what happened to his brothers and he had risen above his circumstances to achieve considerable business success, but he was a hot-tempered person, easy to anger, and as a result he had trouble building lasting relationships.

Whenever this guy talked about his brothers, he cursed them and called them names like fools, and idiots. One day, I asked him why he talked about them that way, and this time, instead of responding with anger, he gave me a glimpse into the real emotion he had been dealing with: "I call them names because they left me, the dirty . . ." he said.

He was still grieving for his brothers because as a young boy, and on into adulthood, he had never allowed himself to deal with his feelings of abandonment and loss. He had masked his grief with anger, and in a sense, that anger had served him well because he had channeled it into positive energy. He used it in his own life to overcome the violence and crime that had killed his brothers. But you can't deny grief its day. It is like water that builds up against a dam. Unless you provide some release for it, the force of it will eventually break through.

The point here is that in the breakaway stage, you have to make the conscious effort to say good-bye to the people and the things you are leaving behind in order to move ahead with your life. You can't just walk away from where you have been and expect to forget it. It is far better to acknowledge its impact on your life, reflect on both the good and bad, say your good-byes, and then move on with confidence that you are ready to make a change for the better.

When I decided to move to Los Angeles, one of the most difficult things I had to do was break up with my longtime girlfriend. Before I made the decision, I had made plans to spend the holidays with her and her family. To my surprise, they had all come to the conclusion that I was going to present her with an engagement ring over the holidays, when in fact I was planning on telling her that I was moving far away without her. It was an extremely uncomfortable and difficult time, believe me. But the fact is that I had to do it and deal with it honestly if I was going to take control of my life and chase my dream. It also made me reflect on just what an impact this decision to move to L.A. was going to have on my life, which brings us to the next stage:

Stage 3: What the Heck Am I Doing Here?

Some psychologists call this the "postdecision stage," but I prefer my label because that's the question that kept nagging me after I arrived in Los Angeles. At first, of course, it was exciting and really cool to find myself living so close to the rich and famous. But after a while it began to sink in that it was close but no cigar for Jake—not to mention no beach house, no mansion, no Ferrari, and no starlets hanging around, either.

This is probably the most difficult stage in the change process, and a lot of people melt down at this point. They give in to the emotional barrage of loneliness, self-pity, and the sense of isolation that can set in. I have a friend who moved around a lot in his twenties and thirties, when he was single and working his way up in his profession. He said that he came to accept that it would take him *at least* two years before he could build up a good circle of friends and feel comfortable and established after each move. He said just knowing that and being aware of it didn't guarantee that he wasn't going to feel lonely from time to time. But he understood that those feelings were a natural part of the process of his climb up the career ladder. That level of understanding helped him deal with his feelings without being overwhelmed by them.

You need to understand, too, that when you enact change in your life, whether it involves moving to a new place, taking a new job, or leaving a relationship, there will be a period in which you wonder, "What the heck am I doing here?" Weakened by loneliness, regret, or self-pity, you will be tempted to second-guess your decision to make a change. During this period, you will probably run up a lot of phone bills calling old friends and family members, and you may try to reestablish contact with those you've already said good-bye to.

A word of caution here: Be careful. It is extremely difficult to go back, once you have made a decision to make a change. When you make a change, you alter the universe. I'm not being cosmic here: Once you decide to change your life, nothing will ever be the same. Places that were once familiar and comfortable will take on an entirely different look and feel. Your former relationships will be altered forever, in some cases for the better, in other cases for the worse.

It is best, then, to continue to look forward, even when you hit this difficult stage. Remember, you can't move up the ladder if you don't let go of the lower rungs and grab those above. I'm sure you know people who seem like they never let go of their high school "glory days." Often, those people don't do well in life because they haven't let go in order to move onward and upward. You have to look ahead to move ahead. So when you hit this stage of the change process, keep in mind that you didn't find what you wanted in the past, so it must lie ahead, in the future.

It's easier to write and talk about coping with change than to actually go through it. I remember driving home from work one day in Los Angeles and thinking that if I was killed in a wreck on the freeway there was nobody in California who could identify my body. Then one day, just as I was really starting to feel sorry for myself, I got what I thought was my first big break, an opportunity to make a name for myself in Hollywood—a chance to stand out from the crowd and be a star. Or so I thought.

It was a typical Hollywood discovery story, only this time it was me instead of Lana Turner at Schwab's. I stopped at a place in Encino to get some vitamins after working out. I was wearing one of those extra-small T-shirts that bodybuilders love. I was pumped up and looking very sporty. A woman started staring at me from the other end of the vitamin aisle, and then she walked up to me, gave me a quick up-and-down appraisal, and asked, "Have you ever heard of the group the Village People?"

I was more of a Jethro Tull fan in those days, but I told the woman I was vaguely aware of the group. I had never seen them perform or read anything about them, but I had heard their music on the radio.

"I'm Susie Frank, and I am head of A&R"—that's Artists and Repertoire—"at Casablanca Records," the woman said. "Have you ever heard of the song 'Macho Man'?"

"Yes," I said.

"Well, you *are* the macho man, and I'm looking for a bodybuilder to pose on stage with the Village People while they perform at a concert next week at the Santa Monica Civic Center."

"Am I on *Candid Camera*?" I asked her.

"Come up to our offices tomorrow and I'll introduce you to some people and we'll pay you a hundred dollars," she said.

I couldn't believe it! The Invisible Man one minute, Macho Man the next.

As she gave me her office address, I was glowing with visions of myself pumped up, rocking and rolling on stage in front of 50,000 screaming fans.

Ladies and gentlemen, Jake Steinfeld . . . and the Village People!!!

I went back to my apartment and telephoned my parents and all my friends. My parents said they would fly in for the show with my sister Nancy, who was only about five years old at the time, but I'm sure she was a *serious* Village People fan.

The next day I went into Casablanca Records and Susie Frank took me in to meet the president, Neil Bogart, who just happened to have the disco diva Donna Summer visiting, so I met her too. They were terrific to me. They gave me a bag full of records and told me to get pumped up for the Saturday-night concert, which was sold out.

The rest of the week dragged by, but finally, Saturday night came and I drove to the Santa Monica Civic Center. I showed my backstage pass to the security guys and they waved me on into a reserved parking spot like I was the king of rock and roll. With my pass around my neck, I went backstage hoping to meet some groupies, but I didn't see any so I got to work. I took off my warm-up suit and stripped down to my gold lamé posing trunks, which the folks at Casablanca had requested. As I was putting tanning oil on to show off my muscles under the lights, the guys from Village People came by and said hello. I hadn't realized they wore such wild costumes. There was an Indian chief, a hard-hat construction worker, a motorcycle guy, and a couple of others. They seemed all right. A little strange, but I told myself you have to expect that with a rock and roll band.

The crowd went nuts when the Village People went out. I could hear the crowd screaming while I was in my dressing room. It was fun actually being backstage at a concert, although I was a little disappointed in the lack of groupies. I had envisioned them being all over the place, and all over me too.

I wanted to look for my folks but I didn't want to blow my big appearance. The night went quickly, and in no time the stage director was telling me it was time for the big "Macho Man" encore.

The lead singer yelled, "How many of you out there think you are macho?"

People in the crowd began waving white handkerchiefs and yelling "Yoo-hoo!"

I thought they were booing.

Then the lead singer said, "We have someone special for you."

The band started cranking into the song, and I walked out. The crowd went crazy. Just as the guys in the group started the first chorus, singing "Macho, macho man . . ." I strutted out on stage with my arms out, flexing my biceps. What a rush! The crowd got even wilder! They were screaming! *Wow, so this is what it feels like to be Mick Jagger,* I thought.

I walked out to the edge of the stage looking for my parents, and also for any ladies that might be interested in meeting the real-life Macho Man later. I spotted my mom and dad and my sister, and they were like three statues. They had very worried looks on their faces. It didn't seem like they were enjoying themselves.

I began to understand why when I did a quick scan of the front rows for the ladies. There were no ladies. It was *all* guys, and a lot of them were wearing a lot of leather. All of these men were waving white handkerchiefs, and it seemed like a lot of them were waving them at me in my skimpy posing shorts.

Suddenly, it dawned on me that the Village People had a unique following—not that there is anything wrong with that, it just wasn't what I had expected. Suddenly, the blood rushed from my face. I was dying. *What have I gotten myself—and my family—into?* As soon as the song was over, Macho Man me rushed backstage, threw on my sweat suit, and went into my dressing room.

I had agreed to meet my parents backstage, thinking they could join me in my moment of triumph. But I was a little shocked. When my parents came backstage to the dressing area, my father was pale. My mother and sister looked at me as if the body snatchers had just returned me.

"Jake, why are all those guys kissing and hugging each other?" my sister asked.

"Son, I think we'd better talk about you going back to college," my father said.

At that point, I thought maybe he was right. The Village People incident would live in comic infamy in my life story. Looking back, I see it as one of the funniest things that ever happened to me.

The Village People experience occurred during what was probably the toughest time in my life up to that point. I felt like a lost puppy. I was trying to make a move that would put me in a position to chase my dream. What I didn't realize then was that I was about to enter one of the most exciting and rewarding stages of the change process:

Stage 4: Life Is an Adventure

Most people are afraid of change because change doesn't come with any guarantees that you will immediately become happier, skinnier, better looking, or richer. In the early stages of change, in fact, you can expect that many of the surprises may not be all that pleasant. At the first sign of a challenge, some people may be tempted to run right back into the security of their comfort zones. That is a mistake.

Remember when you were a teenager and late at night you would get muscle cramps and aches? Your parents told you that you were simply experiencing "growing pains." The same thing happens when you bring about major changes in your life. You will move from the comfort zone to the discomfort zone *temporarily*. Remember that. It is a *temporary* state you pass through in order to grow while improving the overall quality of your life.

Watching my kids, Morgan and Nicky, grow from highly dependent infants to the crawling and "discovery" stages and then into the more independent stages, when they learned to walk and do more things on their own, I could easily see the natural, step-by-step process of physical change. In fact, I guess I am something of an expert on physical change after having trained myself and a lot of other people. I understand very well that to build strength and self-confidence in the physical arena, you have to first tear down muscle and then slowly rebuild it, going through pain and struggle to reach power and strength. But again, that is physical change.

It is often more difficult for us to grasp and accept the same processes when undergoing *emotional* change, struggle, and growth. Even then, it is one thing to say you understand the process of emotional change and an entirely different matter to accept it and live through it. What do many people do when they find themselves feeling lost and confused, lonely and full of doubt during a period of emotional change and growth? The same thing they do when struggling through a physical change and growth period. They look for shortcuts, or easier ways to get through the process. That is a natural reaction, too, an instinctive act of survival and self-preservation, but it is one that you have to deny for your own good.

I noted earlier that there are many sad instances in which someone has soared to a high level of success in the entertainment industry, business, or sports, only to self-destruct. That self-destruction is most often due to the fact that the individual has short-circuited the process of emotional change. The individual has attained rapid success without being prepared for it emotionally and so he or she feels undeserving or ill equipped.

You can't take shortcuts and expect maximum long-term results in bodybuilding or weight training either. In fact, I've seen people seriously hurt themselves and do long-term damage to their bodies by pushing for short-term results. When I moved to L.A. to become a competitive bodybuilder, I definitely discovered my discomfort zone. I put a lot of pressure on myself when I made the move, not only because I left behind my family and friends, but also because I told everyone I wouldn't be back until I was Mr. America. I jumped into it headfirst, but without doing a lot of homework about what it took to reach that level of competition. I had built my body up from a flabby Twinkie repository into 245 pounds of muscle through sheer determination and hard work. I naively thought that was how everyone did it.

The first competition I entered upon arriving in L.A. was the Mr. Teenage Los Angeles contest. As soon as I began training for it in the gyms of L.A., I discovered that I was at a definite disadvantage—one that I had not even dreamed of when I decided to make my move.

The other guys who would be my competition had big thick muscles beyond anything I had seen, other than in the muscle magazines. They were also juiced up, full of energy, working out all day long without seeming to fatigue. I was trying to drop weight while building muscle mass. I'd cut out carbohydrates for the last two weeks before a competition in order to drop my weight. The problem was that carbohydrates supply your body with the energy that fuels both your body and mind. I'd look great, but I dragged my feet and drooled a lot.

It quickly became apparent that there was no way I could maintain my energy level like the other guys. Then I discovered why.

"You'll never make it without steroids, Jake," another competitor advised me.

Steroids? I'd never heard of them back home. I didn't want to believe it was true, but the more I saw of the competitive bodybuilding world, the more I realized it was pumped through and through with steroids. And even though there were no rules at the time against them, I wanted no part of them. They ran against everything I believed about building strength naturally and keeping my body pure. And, I freely admit, I had no interest in sticking needles in my own buttissimo. It's one thing to have a doctor do that in order to stay healthy; it's another thing altogether to be jabbing myself in the rear for trophies.

Because I refused to go for short-term gains by taking drugs now shown to have long-term ill effects, I could not compete with those who used steroids. I found myself standing on stage with the competition, feeling like a lightweight in the land of the giants. I'd be so weak from dieting that I'd be afraid that the air-conditioning fans might blow me off stage. I placed fifth in the Mr. Teenage Los Angeles competition. The guy who won was on steroids. For all of my hard work, I got a plaque the size of a postcard. Then I entered the Mr. Southern California contest and got second place. The guy who got first was on steroids. That was it for me. I wasn't into going for short-term glory at the expense of long-term physical problems. I had gotten into bodybuilding because I wanted to feel good about myself physically and mentally. Using steroids would only have made me feel like I was cheating myself and everybody else.

So in the midst of one difficult change—in fact, the biggest change of my life—I made yet another one. At the time, I felt like I'd been really naive about the realities of bodybuilding. I was shocked and ashamed and down on myself. Looking back, though, I am proud of the decisions I made. I may have been dazed and confused, but my instincts were right.

Sometimes you will make a change to better your life by setting goals for yourself and then come to the realization that your goals are not a good fit. At this critical point, the mistake that many people make is that they decide that making the change was the mistake. No. If you are not happy with your life, change is necessary. *The process of change will often require that you put aside what you may be tempted to go for right now, in order to get what you really want later.*

The realization that I was never going to be Mr. America was a blow to me, but it came at a good time. When I realized the truth about professional bodybuilders, I was already in an advanced level of the change process. I had made a decision to change. I had said good-bye to the life that I'd left behind. I had weathered the initial emotional storms of loneliness and isolation and disorientation, and I had entered this new stage where I had come to see my life as an adventure in which anything could happen.

Suddenly, I found myself open to opportunities of all sorts. This is the period when I got the job at Universal Studios and then befriended Tommy Chong and Cheech Marin. In fact, during this time I began to make other friends and come across all sorts of opportunities. I'll let you in on a little secret here: The key to this stage, the life-is-an-adventure stage, is that having made that change, I was rapidly developing self-confidence and trust in my own ability to handle whatever life presented me with.

When you begin to feel that way about yourself, you become more adventurous and you open yourself up to other people. *Before people will accept you, they have to sense that you accept yourself.* This is a critical rule of PowerLiving. If others are to be comfortable with you, they need to see that you are comfortable with yourself. When you enact change in your life and go after what you want in spite of self-doubt and challenging times, others see that you have bought in to a greater vision for your life, and soon they buy in to it, too. Tommy Chong and Cheech Marin saw that in me and they bought in to it. Even though Womba went down on the cutting-room floor, and I was disappointed about that, the thought of going back to Long Island never seriously tempted me.

I had come to see what sort of life was possible when I stuck with my decision to take control, and I had developed a taste for adventure. That belief in myself and my ability to direct my own life propelled me into the greatest period in the process of change:

Stage 5: Flowin' and Growin'

When you plant a seed or bulb in the fall, it has to weather the difficult conditions of winter before it can begin to grow in the more benevolent conditions of spring. Even then, as its bloom pushes through the soil and into the atmosphere, it has to struggle to survive. But once summer hits, it puts down deep roots that guarantee long-term growth.

This stage is the "summer" of your development in the process of change. You have weathered the most challenging and difficult periods of making the change in your life. You have persevered and pushed through those challenging times and now you have matured and rooted yourself in preparation for long-term growth.

That is not to say that you have entered Camelot, where there are no more dragons to slay and life is beautiful all the time. There will *always* be fresh challenges. There will *always* be setbacks and failures and disappointments in your life. But having mastered your ability to handle change, you are well armed for these dragons. The beauty is that once you have conquered your fear of change, you can always enact change again and again and again. You can handle it because you have learned to believe in your power over your own life.

I don't think it is any coincidence that I met and married Tracey at this stage in my life. I had dated a lot of women up to this point, but it wasn't until I'd grown confident in who I was and where I was going that I had the maturity to attract a woman like her. She was the best thing that happened to me in this period, but there were many others. My business flourished. I began to get more and more opportunities in television and movies, and I built a large network of long-lasting and rewarding friendships.

Once you have reached this stage, you have learned to *expect* success because you believe that you have earned it and deserve it. Change has become a tool. You no longer fear it because you have mastered the ability to handle it. Sure, there will be more challenges. But you now have the confidence to handle them. It is also important that you take time at this stage to be thankful for having come this far, and for the blessings you have received.

I try to do that now. I try, too, to acknowledge that none of these great things and experiences would have happened if I had not gone through the other stages of the process. None of it would have happened if I had not decided that I *had* to make a change. None of it would have happened if I hadn't let go of the life I'd been leading and reached for a higher rung. None of it would have happened if I'd given in to my loneliness, fears, and frustration and gone back to Long Island. None of it would have happened if I hadn't understood that in order to grow I was going to experience growing pains.

And none of it will happen to you, either, unless you decide to make a change to go after what *you* want for your life! Understand that change is vital to your long-term growth and development. You have to enact change. You have to learn how to handle all that comes with it. And you have to welcome change as your most valuable tool for reaching your dreams and goals. That is Power-Living!

POWERLIVING
LESSON NO. 11

Commit and Get It!

Shortly after I moved to California to go after my dream of being a professional bodybuilder, my father—you'll remember I told you my folks had moved to California too—tried to turn me into a salesman, which is what he did for a living. He sold advertising for his local magazine and he did well at it. He thought I had the makings of a good advertising salesman, too, but mostly, he was worried that I didn't have any concrete goals for my life at that point.

Needless to say, he didn't think much of my talk about becoming a professional bodybuilder, even though he had bought me my first weight set. In the list of preferred careers for oldest sons, professional bodybuilder was not even ranked. He thought I needed to get my feet more firmly planted in a real job, so he asked me to work with him on a trial basis. He even set me up to go on a sales call to one of his clients, a florist. Now, I didn't know it then, but my father had tipped the florist off and promised him a free ad if he would play along by making it tough on me to make the sale. My father figured if the florist played hard to get, my competitive juices would kick in and I would enjoy the challenge of "winning" him over so much that I'd give up on being Mr. America.

Guess what? There was one major problem with my father's little scheme. He didn't understand that I had no *commitment* to being a salesman. He was gambling that hidden somewhere on my DNA chain was a Willy Loman salesman gene waiting to be plugged in. It wasn't there. I admired my father's sales skills and I appreciated the hard work it took to be a salesman, but it was just not enough of a physical activity for me at that time in my life. I'd built my body into something I was proud of and that's where my focus and commitment were.

I respected my dad, so I agreed to go along with his salesman-for-a-day plan, even though it meant putting on a suit. I have never been much for wearing a suit. Suits were not made for guys like me. Piano covers were made for guys like me. When I used to wear a suit, it looked like somebody had tried to turn the refrigerator into a men's department mannequin. People would see me stuffed into a suit and tie and call the bomb squad and report an explosion about to occur. *Stand back, he's gonna blow.*

I did it for my father, though. I got a suit and tie on and tucked my dad's magazine under my arm and drove to the florist's shop. I walked in and asked to meet with the owner. He came out and I said, "Hi, I'm Jake Steinfeld. I would like to offer you the inside front cover for eight hundred fifty dollars."

He looked at it for a second and said, "No, thanks."

I said, "Okay, thanks." And left.

When I returned to my father's office, he was waiting proudly at the front door. "Here's my boy, how did it go?" he asked, thinking that his little scheme had worked.

"The guy at the florist shop said no," I reported.

"Of course he said no. I asked him to give you a hard time but to take the ad anyway. I was testing you. You putz."

My father saw then that I was not committed to being an ad salesman, and that I would never have the drive to be successful at it. He realized that I was not buying in to his dream for me. He understood what many parents come to understand: that right or wrong, their children sometimes need to find their own way.

It's funny, because there were all sorts of people who thought I could be a good salesman, and very few who thought I had any future as a bodybuilder. In a way, of course, they were right. I never became Mr. America, and today in many ways I am a salesman, just as all entrepreneurs are salespeople. I am an incredibly relentless salesman when it comes to selling the brand of Body by Jake because I am committed to that.

Topping the Tank

One of the greatest measures of your ability to go after what you want in life is the level of commitment you show. The commitments you make to yourself and to others, and the energy you invest in keeping those commitments, determine how successful you are in your drive to achieve your Ultimate Goal. The upward spiral of your life from one goal to the next is governed by your ability to make and keep commitments. This is how you establish control over your own life.

You may have dreams and a plan to go after your Ultimate Goal. You may have the courage to face your fears. You may understand that failure is merely a stepping-stone to success. But until you are fully committed you don't have the gas to get you down the street and up the hill and through the ditches and over the barricades to where you need to go.

Commitment is the only thing that makes you a serious player in this game. It makes you *relentless* in going after what you want in life. It gives you the drive and energy to stay on the path to your dreams. Without it, you can easily fall by the wayside.

Commitment is the fuel that drives your dreams into reality. It is the difference between someone who is a successful person who makes things happen in his or her life and the person who just coasts or drifts along. I was talking to my old buddy David Parret the other day and we were joking about playing against each other in basketball when we went to different high schools. "Jake, you were the kind of guy who didn't just dive after loose balls, you would dive after the ball if someone was holding it in their hands," he said. "You would do anything you had to do to get what you wanted then, and now too."

David is right. When I am committed to getting something I want, I dive after it. I believe in relentless commitment. I go after what I want as if the buzzer is going to sound any second and end the game. I may run out of time, but I will never run out of commitment.

The Clock Is Ticking

I believe that we have only so much time on this planet, and so I live with one eye on my goals and the other on the clock. Every morning, I get up around four-thirty and I hear that clock ticking as soon as I'm on my feet. From the minute I awaken, it's me against that clock. I try to see how much I can get accomplished before breakfast by getting my workout in and making some important phone calls while also getting in time with my wife and kids. I love getting a jump on the day like that.

Every morning I make a list of the goals I want to accomplish that day. Some of them are "red flag" goals, challenges I need to address in my businesses or in personal matters such as malfunctioning household appliances. Not a day goes by that there aren't things on the list related to new projects or ideas that have come to me to expand the brand Body by Jake. I don't want there to be a day when I haven't at least spent time looking for new ways to grow and challenge myself and my businesses.

Making the Leap

Here is my Three-Step Formula for Committing to a Better Life:

1. Don't get ready.
2. Don't get set.
3. Just GO!

Did you ever notice that the word "goal" starts with "go"? To go after what you want, you have to commit to it. The mountain climber W. H. Murray was an adventurer with a poetic spirit. He would quote the German scientist and philosopher Johann Wolfgang von Goethe when committing himself to his expeditions in the Himalayas: "Whatever you can do, or dream you can, begin it. Boldness has genius, power, and magic in it!"

I've found that when I want to get something accomplished but I am not certain how to go about doing it, if I just commit to it, I find a way. Sometimes, that's the best way to get rolling. A lot of my friends are starting families these days and one of the things I've noticed is that they are no longer repeating what used to be a very common refrain: "We want kids, we're just waiting for the right time." They have discovered that there is no perfect time for starting a family. There is no alarm that goes off and says: You have enough money in the bank. Your career is at a perfect stage. You have enough rooms in the house. You have seen and done all you want to do as a couple without children so . . . START A FAMILY NOW!

Sorry, it doesn't work that way. But you find that once you start having children, you discover ways to make everything else work. You really don't have any choice once you make that commitment! But how many people waste years of their lives getting set, getting more ready, and getting even readier and more set . . . but never getting off and going?

If you make the leap by committing, you will find a way. One of my mottoes is "Go Big or Stay Home," which means if you can't commit, don't bother.

I recently read about another guy who follows that philosophy. When Bill Gates, the founder of Microsoft, was still in his twenties and trying to get his business started, he learned about a company in New Mexico that was building an early version of the personal computer and was looking for an operating system for its product. Gates contacted the company and told them that he had such a program and arranged to be their supplier.

Bill Gates didn't have an operating system at that point. But once he had committed to delivering one, he had the drive and energy to develop one. His operating system became the foundation for what is now one of the most profitable and valuable companies in the world.

Commitment Is Contagious

When I commit to something, I get emotional and excited about it. I've found that when I get emotional and excited, it is contagious. If you are truly positive and enthusiastic about what you are doing, whatever it is, you'll find others are drawn to that and they are far more willing to buy in to you and your dreams.

When I am promoting my businesses, I feel like I can sell anybody on them because I believe in them. The difference between now and back when I was selling for my father is that today I sell products and services and a brand that I am fully committed to. No, I'm not just committed—I am *relentless* in going after the goals that I have set for myself and my businesses. Today, I am involved in expanding my brand and building my businesses through infomercials, the Home Shopping Network, FiT TV, a television sitcom, a movie, a new magazine, and this book. Is that relentless, or what?

The Goal Has Got to Be Right for You

You have to be relentless in pursuing all of your goals. That's what true commitment is all about. If you can't work up the energy and the commitment to be relentless, then you have obviously chosen the wrong goals and you need to find new ones in order to truly enjoy your life. Was my lack of enthusiasm about selling advertising space in my father's magazine due to a lack of a commitment? No, my lack of a commitment was only a symptom of the real challenge, which was that it was the wrong *goal*. My father wanted me to be an advertising salesman. I didn't. It was his goal, not mine. That's why he could commit to it and I couldn't.

I'll give you proof. One of my primary goals right now is to make my new magazine a success. Since I was fifteen I've read muscle magazines and health and fitness magazines and I now have the opportunity to do something better with my own. About a year ago, I went to New York and I pitched the idea for a *Body by Jake* magazine to several of the biggest publishing companies in the country. Many were interested, and I chose Hachette Filipacchi Magazines Inc. because I really hit it off with the president and CEO, David Pecker. He was just as excited about the prospect as I was.

Then, shortly after I signed the deal with Hachette, I received a telephone call from the head of their advertising department. He said he wasn't sure the magazine concept was going to work for me because his salespeople weren't finding a great deal of enthusiasm among key advertisers. You might be tempted to think that life was playing a little trick with me. Here I am, the guy who once walked away from the opportunity to sell ads for his father's publication because I was not committed to the concept. Now, it's *my* magazine, and it appears that Hachette's salespeople weren't fully committed to the concept, or at least that they haven't been committed enough to sell it to others.

Believe me, that went through my head as I mulled over the Hachette executive's phone call. This time, however, *I* was fully committed to making *my* magazine work and I was prepared to be relentless in accomplishing that goal because it was *my goal*. It was something I believed in. I called the Hachette advertising guy back.

"You know, if you need to drum up advertiser interest in the *Body by Jake* magazine, then I think you need to call in a drummer who has the most at stake in its success, the guy who is fully committed and prepared to be relentless—ME!"

A few days later I hit the ground running in New York City, L.A., Detroit, and Chicago. I visited advertising buyers for cosmetics, food, cars—you name it—and I was relentless. And as a result we had a great launch.

I don't blame Hachette's salespeople. They just needed to see how excited and committed David Pecker and I were to making it work. And now they are pumped up too! You can't expect anyone else to be as committed to your dreams and goals as you are. And if you don't show people that you are prepared to be relentless in your commitment, you can't expect them to sign on to your dream. But when you do show that you are fully committed, others will be drawn to you because everyone wants to back a winner. Those who are relentlessly committed to their goals and dreams are already winners anyway because they are living life to its greatest potential! PowerLiving!

Bracing for Commitment

While I think commitment is critical, I think it is also true that you cannot *make* yourself feel commitment. You have to believe in what you are doing to work up the relentless drive of commitment. When I am not committed to something, I can be equally relentless about getting out of it. When I was thirteen years old, I had to get braces. I had the heavy-metal mouth treatment. I could set off airport metal detectors just by walking through the terminal. I hated those braces. They not only hurt, but I was at a particularly awkward stage where I had an Afro, a yes-no mustache (a little hair there, none there, etc.), and a voice that couldn't find a tone to stick with. The braces were not helping the self-image at all.

One day I was playing Police Boys Club basketball and I got hit in the mouth for about the tenth straight time. All that metal was just shredding my gums. I bled so bad I had to go home and I was so angry about all the pain and torment the braces were causing me, I went downstairs to the basement, got out a pair of pliers, yanked the braces off, and threw them in the garbage!

For the next two weeks, every time the orthodontist's office called, I pretended to be my father and told them that my son was ill but that he would call in for an appointment as soon as he recuperated. I got away with that for a while, but then one night at the dinner table, I forgot to cover my mouth when I started laughing because my father had tossed an egg roll at one of my brothers for screwing up. My mother noticed that the flash had gone out of my smile.

"Where are your braces?" she demanded.

I told her the orthodontist had decided I didn't need them. She didn't buy it. My parents were furious, of course, and I think I mowed lawns until I was thirty-five in order to pay them back for the cost of the braces that I yanked and trashed. But they certainly saw that I was not committed to wearing them, and they never sent me back to the orthodontist. My parents knew me well. When I don't feel committed to something, I can't fake it.

Recently I was working on a live presentation for a fifteen-city promotional campaign for FiT TV, but I wasn't sold on the message that we wanted to deliver. I wasn't getting the concept, and as a result, I couldn't come across on the promotion in an effective manner.

Finally, we took a break and I talked with Steve Lentz, president of FiT TV, and Bob Hammer, who had designed the presentation, and we hashed out the meaning of the message until it was something that I thought I could stand behind. Once I had committed to it, my whole approach changed. I got the job done immediately then. Afterward, both Steve and Bob told me that they had always felt that I was such a natural-born salesman that I could sell any product. "But today, we learned that you have to believe in something before you can sell it."

Committed to Survival at Sea

One of the early things I did in television that really helped build the Body by Jake brand was the *Fitness Break by Jake* on Cable News Network. Ted Turner had read an article on me in *People* magazine and he wanted to make the network more user-friendly. I didn't even know what CNN was at that point. He said think about it and call me. So I came up with the concept where I could show off my personality as well as my fitness expertise with the *Fitness Break by Jake,* which was only 60 seconds long.

Ted wasn't willing to pay me much to do the fitness breaks, but we both knew that the long-term benefits to me of appearing on CNN would be huge. It's important to remember that not every step you take along the way to your long-term goal is going to carry immediate rewards, but if you are committed, you will be willing to take those small steps that will reap you big rewards down the road. In the Bible it says, "Don't despise the day of small beginnings."

Everybody seems to be looking for the big score, instead of building for success. I could have told Ted to buzz off because he didn't want to pay me a lot. Sometimes it isn't about the money; it is about the experience you are gaining, which will take you to the next level.

I worked my buttissimo off on the fitness breaks. We had great locations in Malibu, Beverly Hills, or the Hollywood Hills and shot two hundred of those 60-second spots in three days. In four years, we did eight hundred of them, and that exposure on CNN helped expand the Body by Jake brand enormously. They were so popular that they led to lucrative deals for me and my company to do home videos, exercise books, and hundreds of personal appearances.

To this day, I see the success of my businesses as springing from those spots on CNN. They were an unbelievably important step in my career. Back when I was doing them, they weren't bringing in a lot of money, but they helped me see that the sacrifice and hard work were going to pay off someday in a big way. That early commitment was so strong, it actually made me take on one of my greatest fears—seasickness. A CNN marketing executive called me one day and said he had come up with the idea of taking some of his top CNN advertising clients and their spouses on a "fitness cruise" to promote the network. They wanted me to go on the cruise and to meet and talk to people as well as lead daily workouts on the boat.

My immediate response was to bend over and hold my stomach. I'm a healthy guy, but my sea legs are notoriously shaky. "How about a nice landlubber bowling party, or a stickball game? That's more my thing," I suggested to the marketing guy.

Then he pulled out the big guns.

"Ted really wants you to do this for him, Jake," he said.

"Oh, man, I'm starting to feel woozy already," I replied. But I said I would think about it.

I talked to Tracey that night and she told me she had spent an entire college semester at sea, traveling around the world, and she had never gotten sick. "You hardly feel any movement on those big cruise ships," she said.

I went to sea for CNN. As we departed from Miami on the cruise ship, they held a cocktail party in my honor. Although it was billed as a CNN Body by Jake Fitness Cruise, there was a lot of partying going on. It wasn't the Love Boat, but it wasn't a funeral barge either—at least, not for anyone other than me. I definitely had a near-death experience on this cruise.

We had hardly cleared the harbor when I started to feel queasy. It showed, too. "You don't get seasick do you, Jake? You look a little pale," said one of the advertisers I'd been talking to.

I knew I was in trouble, so I excused myself and headed for my room. The Puke Monster found me there. He sent me to the porcelain altar, where I knelt for an hour or so. At that point, it was either go to bed and spend the entire cruise weekend in sick bay, or test my commitment to making this work and muscle my way past the Puke Monster. I washed up and returned to the party. I still looked so bad people thought I was joking. I was like a wet rag.

Word spread that I was seasick, and that didn't help a bit. One guy did give me a seasickness patch to wear, another gave me some Dramamine, and a third person brought me some crackers, but a whole lot of other people decided this was the time for them to share their personal seasickness stories with me.

I begged Tracey to get me off the boat before I went overboard to swim with the fishies, but she told me I'd get over it in a while. I never did really get over it, but I decided that it wasn't going to get between me and my goal for this cruise. There were a lot of important people aboard, and it was a great opportunity for me to develop relationships that could prove valuable down the road. I could not afford to jump ship or to spend the entire weekend heaving over the side. I pulled it together and got on with business.

Not only did I find my sea legs, I led four different exercise classes over each of the next two days. Now *that* is commitment. When you are truly committed, neither rain, nor sleet, nor the Puke Monster can distract you from your goals. You become relentless in getting up and going after what you want. You always know what needs to be done and you always figure out a way to do it, because you know that the rewards ahead are far greater than the struggle and the challenges you are facing.

The Uncommitted Life

A few years ago I had an office manager who was a wonderful guy, but he suffered from a terrible lack of commitment. Like 95 percent of the population of Los Angeles, he really wanted to be an actor, but he hadn't made a commitment to that, and as a result, he wasn't getting much work in acting. He also wanted to work for me to make ends meet, but he didn't have much commitment to that job either. Oh, he was good with people on the telephone and he was a pleasant person to have around, but he did only the minimum required to hang on to his job. He was often late to work, too, which he would always try to cover up, even when I had nearly run over him as he ran from the bus stop to the office.

I liked him personally, and I wanted to see him succeed at something. Unfortunately, I was more committed to his success with my business than he was. As my company grew, so did the demands on him, and he wasn't willing to grow too. I became concerned that he was wasting my time and his time, and if acting was what he really wanted to do, I thought he had better go after it with everything he had. I told him that, and he understood and set off to chase his dream.

Here's one last helpful way to understand commitment. The next time you throw all of your healthy eating rules out the window and go for a double cheeseburger and chocolate milkshake, consider this: Your meal would not have been possible without

1. A dairy cow
2. A beef cow

While each of them makes a valuable contribution to your meal, there is a huge difference in their level of participation. The dairy cow merely *contributed* to the meal, while the beef cow was *fully committed*!

So, the next time you decide that your life isn't going where you want it to go, ask yourself, "Where's the beef? Where is the commitment?"

TWO FINAL WORDS

Don't Quit!

Body by Jake Enterprises had been up and running only a short time when I received a telephone call from some people at a giant athletic-gear maker. No, they didn't want to market a Big Jake basketball shoe. (I wonder why not?) In fact, they wanted to buy something from me. They wanted to buy one of my start-up company's few assets.

Their representatives said they were willing to pay me for this asset, and their offer came at a time when my cash flow was more like a trickle. I gave their offer some serious thought, but in the end I decided that this company's interest in this asset only confirmed what I already knew—that I had something extremely valuable and that we should hang on to it.

If this big company, one of the most competitive and well-run companies in the nation, wanted this asset, then I figured the asset would be even more valuable down the road. It has been. The two final words I have for you in this chapter *are* that asset, my trademarked motto: "Don't Quit!"

In the preceding chapters, I've given you the tools you need to go after your dreams and goals, but if you throw those tools down and run at the first sign of a challenge, they will do you no good at all. You can't quit. Ever.

Don't Even Think About It

I have to confess that another reason I didn't sell my trademarked motto was that it has been one of my most prized possessions for a very long time. Although I was a fat kid, I was always a good athlete and that helped me overcome a lot of challenges. I was pretty confident about my athletic ability, but that confidence was seriously shaken in eighth grade at Baldwin Junior High School. They held tryouts for the basketball team and I went through that week without putting out a whole lot of effort because I *knew* I was going to make the team. I loved basketball and I thought I was good at it. I was not really tall but I had a lot of bulk. Sort of a short-stack Shaq.

When the roster of those picked for the team was posted in the gym, I sauntered up confidently with my buddies, already talking about what number I wanted on my home and away jerseys. But their names were on the roster, and mine wasn't. I was stunned. In fact, I was so sure there had been a mistake, I ripped the roster off the wall to see if my name was on the other side. It wasn't.

I hadn't made the team! I am not exaggerating when I tell you that I have never in my life felt as low as I felt at that point. A lot of my self-esteem was based on my athletic ability in those days. I may have been overweight, and I may have had a speech impediment, but I was a *jock*. Well, the wind was definitely taken out of my sails.

I wanted to go hide, I was so embarrassed. I didn't want to ever show my face again. But then, just a few days later, a friend, a girl who lived down the street, gave me a poem that changed my entire attitude about life. I wasn't exactly a poem-reading kind of guy back then, but this one had so much resonance for my life at that point that it really got to me. It's not Emily Dickinson. It's not even Neil Diamond, but it works for me and I know it will work for you too.

It's called "Don't Quit!"

> When things go wrong as they sometimes will,
> When the road you're trudging seems all uphill,
> When the funds are low, and the debts are high,

And when you want to smile, but you have to sigh,
  When care is pressing you down a bit,
    Rest if you must, but do not quit.

  Life is queer, with its twists and turns
  As every one of us sometimes learns.
    And many a failure turns about
  When he might have won had he stuck it out.
  Don't give up, though the pace seems slow.
  You may succeed with another blow.

  Success is failure turned inside out—
  The silver tint of the clouds of doubt.
  And you never can tell how close you are.
    It may be near when it seems so far.
  So stick to the fight when you're hardest hit.
  It's when things seem worst that you must not quit.

I memorized this poem immediately after my neighbor gave it to me. I recited it at dinnertime, and my dad was so impressed that he said if I was still determined to make the team, he would help me. That's what happens when you demonstrate your determination to other people. They sign on. They join the team. They buy in to your dream. My dad bought in by putting up a basketball hoop in the backyard so I could practice, practice, practice. And I did.

He took our train set off a big piece of plywood in the basement and cut a backboard out of it. I played basketball in the rain, the sleet, and the snow. I played after school and into the night with my little brothers rebounding for me. I made the basketball team the next year, and, believe it or not, I became the team captain and a starter all through high school. Before every game, I recited the poem "Don't Quit!" to myself.

I've learned that if you don't quit, you will win out. In this book, I've given you the tools you need to get your life on the right track. So, now it is up to you. You can do it, if you *Don't Quit!*

When all else is said and done, these two words are probably the most important words in the vocabulary of success. Most of you probably think of them in the context of pursuing your goals and dreams. You are correct; quitting is not an option if you are going to build a better life. But you must also keep this motto in mind when you achieve one of your goals, or even when you have reached the point of living within your Ultimate Goal.

Don't Quit, Spin!

I have seen a lot of people achieve a goal and then sit back and rest on their laurels or decide that they've accomplished all they need to accomplish. But when you sit down, you tend to disappear from view. My advice then is, *Don't Quit!* Instead, *Spin!*

Let's take a little spin right now to show you what I mean:

- A fat kid with a stutter in a middle-class family on Long Island changes both his body shape and his self-image one day at a time by devoting himself to a regular routine of exercise.
- Once he grasps that he can control his body, the kid begins to understand that it is up to him to take control of the rest of his life. The stutter fades away, and after some soul-searching he moves to Los Angeles at the age of nineteen to become Mr. America.
- Then, he makes a major leap up the ladder of maturity when he has the self-respect and self-control to abandon his dream of being Mr. America after that dream goes sour. He realizes that the use of steroids to build strength runs counter to his values regarding true physical fitness. He begins working out an actress friend who wants to get in shape for a commercial. Since she dislikes weights, he improvises with a broom and a couple of kitchen chairs to get her into shape.
- The actress spreads the word that she now has a Body by Jake, and soon all of Hollywood is looking for the former fat kid from Long Island and his magic bodybuilding broom. He spins his successful work with the actress, the broom, and the kitchen chairs and creates the personal fitness training industry.
- The Trainer to the Stars spins his success in that one-man operation, as well as his newly established Hollywood contacts

and notoriety, into the low-paying but high-profile *Fitness Break by Jake* on the emerging Cable News Network, enhancing its programming and the value of his Body by Jake brand.

- The CNN *Fitness Break by Jake* guy spins into videos and books, a fitness show that goes from syndication to ESPN, and then into a product-licensing and marketing company involved in a series of infomercials that sell hundreds of millions of dollars' worth of fitness products.

- The success of these Body by Jake products spins into the creation of the sitcom *Big Brother Jake* on the Family Channel.

- Spinning upward with the popularity of Body by Jake television programming, he creates FiT TV, a health and fitness cable television network in partnership with International Family Entertainment, Reebok, and TCI.

- The Body by Jake brand attracts even more lucrative offers from the television, movie, and publishing worlds, which he spins into a major book deal.

- The broom and kitchen chairs are placed on display in the Smithsonian Institution in Washington, D.C. (Hey, it could happen!)

You Spin You Win

I took you for a spin through my life not to impress you with what a wonderful and successful person I am, but to show you how a regular guy—a guy without a college degree—was able to build a great life by telling himself "Don't Quit" in both the challenging times *and* in times when success came his way.

Don't Quit when you are fighting to get where you want to go in life, and when you get there, Don't Quit in your drive to better your life and the lives of those around you. Instead, tap back into your imagination, create new and even higher goals, and spin each success into even greater accomplishment.

I believe ordinary people can lead *extra*ordinary lives by relentlessly chasing their dreams and goals. You can do it by facing your fears, by seeing failure as merely part of the process of success, and by being committed to your goals. I believe also that those who reach the highest levels of happiness and success are those ordinary people who never stop spinning one success into another.

When I talk about spinning I'm not referring to the "spin" that politicians put on things, or to the spinning on stationary bicycles that is all the rage in fitness centers around the country. In my use of the word, spinning refers to the practice of using each success as a foundation for continuous achievement throughout your lifetime.

Never put limits on yourself. Always stop to savor each success and to be thankful for it and for the talents, hard work, and good fortune that brought it to you. Then, look to see what new opportunities have opened up for you and go after them with all of the enthusiasm and energy that you possess.

By always challenging yourself to meet goals that are neither too difficult nor too easy for your abilities, you create a life in which you are always spinning from one success to the next. You will have challenges. You will have to face your fears, move past failures, and deal with changes. But when you put a positive spin on your life, you will be able to handle all of these challenges.

Spinning Your Wheels

Far too many people spin their wheels rather than spinning their successes. They may achieve a goal now and then, and for some reason they think that's it, they've had their quota of success. It doesn't work that way. If you get only a taste of success and walk away, you'll miss the banquet that awaits. You should aspire to a life that is one long continuous upward spiral of success leading to opportunities that bring even more success.

Remember, though, that life is not about having a luxury car, drinking the finest wines, or living in a forty-room mansion. Those things are fine if you can acquire them without losing track of the most important things. A friend of mine recently attended a "success" seminar attended by more than six hundred people. It was one of those motivational seminars for people searching for more meaning in their lives. The vast majority of the people there were financially successful. Many were entrepreneurs who had built businesses from nothing but their determination and hard work. But many of them were also extremely unhappy people because in their narrowly focused drive to create wealth and security, they had neglected their relationships.

They had achieved their goals, but when they'd reached them they looked around and discovered they were alone. They had no one to share their successes with. There were many sad stories at this meeting of "successful" people because so many had made a critical mistake when they set their goals. They had neglected their hearts. A forty-room mansion can be just as empty as a studio apartment, if you have no one to share your life with.

The way to happiness and fulfillment, the real measure of success, is in continuously challenging your mind while never neglecting what is closest to your heart. Acquiring wealth and security might be part of your dream, but what is most important is spinning success so that the quality of your life gets better and better.

Do you know what my success in business has done? It has made the quality of my life richer because it has allowed me to set my own schedule. Every year I spend an entire month on vacation with my wife and children. When I am not traveling I make it a point to have every meal of the day with my family, whenever it is possible. I have worked hard to build my businesses and my career, but I work hardest at building a strong family foundation. I've spun my success as an entrepreneur so that I now have more opportunities to spend time with those who mean the most to me. That is what building success upon success is all about.

Success is not a final goal, it is a lifestyle. I have a hard time with people who say, "My goal is to make a million dollars"—or ten million or a hundred million—"and then retire at the age of thirty-five"—or forty-five or fifty-five. What sort of goal is that? I can't imagine retiring because I am having too much fun doing what I do. If retiring means not using my talents and enthusiasms . . . if retiring means sitting the rest of my life at poolside or in a fishing boat, count me out. Especially the fishing boat.

What did I start out with? It sure wasn't a lot of money. The only silver spoon at our house was kept in a display cabinet. My hidden asset, though, was my belief that anything was possible. I have made a career out of spinning small successes into bigger ones, and bigger successes into even greater achievements. That doesn't mean that I haven't made mistakes or that I haven't had failures or setbacks. The secret is that I keep pushing ahead, always ready to spin away from defeat and look for new ways to grow and succeed.

I could have been content to be the celebrity trainer to the stars or to create the personal fitness training industry, and believe me, I had a great business that was an incredible amount of fun. But that success only made me hungrier for more, so when opportunities arose to endorse products and to market my own line of fitness products, I spun into that field and created my own company, which led to television, radio, and movie and publishing projects. Always spinning, spinning, spinning.

We all have opportunities for success, but in order to attract success, you have to believe that you deserve it. It is a matter of seizing opportunity, of making your own luck. I worked out with weights. I had big shoulders, good abs and arms. How did that lead to my owning a multi-million-dollar business—my licensing company, my magazine, my infomercials and movie deals? Spinning, said the spider to the fly.

I know a great many people who have managed success well by building tiny strands of success into a life's web of achievement. They are people who began as actors and became directors and producers and the owners of studios. They never rested on their laurels. They always reached higher and higher.

A key to spinning one success into another is never to abandon what brought you success in the first place. Never forget who you are and what has worked for you. I have had opportunities to endorse products outside the fitness field, but I prefer to stick with what I know, and to build upon my expertise within the motivation and fitness field. That is how I manage my successes.

When you dare to dream and have the courage to pursue those dreams, you become a one-person hurricane, pulling in opportunities from all around you while elevating your life and the lives of those close to you. I've discovered that when you put your life into an upward spin by living out of your imagination, setting goals, going after them step by step, and committing yourself to relentlessly going after them in spite of fears, failures, or setbacks, the world will rise up to celebrate your success with you.

But if you give in to your fears and back away from success, you can be swallowed up. I have known people who did not manage success well, people who did not welcome it and did not see each success as a gift to be enjoyed and then built upon. I've known people who feared success or were so obsessed with it that it destroyed them. I have a producer friend who had a "small" movie that became a major hit. At first, he did not know how to handle his success. I will never forget going to his office to congratulate him just after it had been announced that his first picture was the number one box-office hit in its first week in theaters. I thought he would be on the ceiling celebrating, but instead, he was sitting in a dark room with his head in his hands. He told me he was deeply depressed.

"Are you out of your mind?" I asked him.

"How am I ever going to match this success?" he said.

It was my turn to be floored. Where was the celebration? Where was the joy in *this* journey?

I wanted to hit him over the head with a rolled-up copy of *The Hollywood Reporter*. Instead I tried to pull him out of this fear-of-success panic attack. I told him he shouldn't worry about having to repeat or match this movie's commercial success. Instead, he should savor it, and then look to what other great opportunities this would open up for him and his company. I told him he should continue to make the finely crafted movies that he loved, and if they too were embraced by the public that would be fine. I'm glad to say that my friend is now back on track, tremendously successful, and enjoying his life.

Balance in life means that you don't try to control the rhythms of life, you instead control your response to them. You accept success as well as failures, defeats, and hard times as part of the natural ebb and flow. You learn what you can from each part of the cycle while always remaining on alert for your next opportunity to ride an upward wave.

My friend the producer panicked at his own success. He lost his equilibrium momentarily when his life took a leap. You have to be prepared for success too.

Steven Spielberg began his professional career as a television director and worked his way up from directing small and creative movies like *Duel* and *Sugarland Express* to blockbusters like *Jaws* and *Close Encounters* and *E.T.* Slowly, he moved upward from those commercial successes to movies that were more artistic and thoughtful, such as *Empire of the Sun, The Color Purple,* and *Schindler's List.*

He did not escape criticism. While Wiels certainly has felt the impact of the criticism, he has remained in balance and continues to keep his life on an upward spiral by using even criticism as a motivation to reach higher and higher. He understands that life is not about success or failure, and you need to understand that, too. You too will experience both success and failure, criticism and praise, I can guarantee you that. Life is about being in command, no matter what happens to you. It is about believing in your own ability to continuously build a life guided by your dreams and goals in spite of your circumstances, your good or bad fortune, or your successes or failures. If you believe in your ability to spin your own story, then success, no matter how you measure it, is inevitable.

Success has little to do with what things or accomplishments you have accumulated at the end of your time on earth. It has everything to do with what sort of person you have become, what sort of life you have lived, along the way.

Each success and each setback is part of the continuum; each offers something to build upon. If you master the art of spinning, you will always find a way to move forward and upward to greater achievement.

Push-Pull-and-Spin

One of the reasons for my success as a fitness motivator was that I was good at finding the best way to motivate each person I trained. Some people work better with negative motivation: "Come on, let's go for twenty. What? Just ten? Okay, I guess you don't care about that swimsuit scene."

Other people respond better to positive motivation: "You're looking good. You're doing great! Keep it up!"

These two types of motivation reflect the fact that you can be either *pushed* toward something or *pulled* toward it.

Most successful people use both forms of motivation, depending on the situation, but the really successful people are those who have learned to spin one success into another so that their lives are a continuous upward spiral. For them, goals are like magnets that pull them higher and higher to greater accomplishments that make both their lives and the lives of those around them better.

Spinning success has worked for me, a former fat kid from Long Island. It has worked for my buddy Wiels, a shy guy whose application to the USC Film School was turned down twice. It worked for Bette Midler, who has had to overcome hard times in Hollywood. It worked for Harrison Ford, probably the biggest leading man in movies today, who admits he got beat up a lot in high school and then had to pay his dues by building bookshelves and back decks for the stars.

It has also worked for a whole lot of other very successful people whose names may not be up in lights but who nevertheless have overcome hardships or hard times and gone on to lead fulfilling and happy lives doing what they love to do.

It will work for you too.

Making Your Own Luck

There is no doubt that luck, or good fortune, plays a role in your ability to live in an upward spiral. I've been lucky, but I believe that luck is not a matter of chance, it is a matter of being prepared for opportunities when they present themselves. Never forget that it is up to each of us to create our own luck. You don't win the lottery unless you go down to the store and buy the ticket, do you? So who put you in that position to win? You did.

Not that I recommend that you bet on the lottery. The odds are much better if you bet on yourself, on your talents, your intellect, your drive.

How do you make your own luck? How do you spin success upon success? Don't Quit! Live powerfully instead!

When you feel like you aren't getting anywhere in life, Don't Quit.

Believe that you can achieve!

When you feel as though you will never overcome your circumstances, Don't Quit.

Flex your imagination!

When you feel like your get-up-and-go got up and went, Don't Quit.

Go for your goals!

When you can't see the way, Don't Quit. Create a plan.

Get in the flow!

When you feel like you can't get it done on your own, Don't Quit.

Go to your Go-To People!

When you are tempted to take a path that just doesn't feel right, don't take it, and Don't Quit.

Build your brand value instead!

When you can't make up your mind, or you aren't sure about taking a risk, Don't Quit.

Decide to succeed!

When the trolls under the bed and in your mind are holding you back, Don't Quit.

Face your fears!

When you try something and fail, Don't Quit. Be like Womba instead.

Don't look back at the doors that are closing. Look for those that are opening!

When you are having a difficult time dealing with changes in your life, Don't Quit.

Make a change and make it work!

When you find yourself losing ground on your goals, Don't Quit.

Commit and get it!

I've given you the tools. Now it is up to you to put them to work. I know you can do it. If I can, you can. If Wiels can, you can. If Harrison and Bette and Priscilla can do it, you can, too. We've got nothing on you!

So what are you hanging around for? Get to it! I'll be right here, cheering you on! PowerLiving—it's the only way to live!

INDEX

About the Author

JAKE STEINFELD is one of the world's great motivators in personal development and physical conditioning for optimum performance. The pioneer of the personal fitness training field and creator of FiT TV, the twenty-four-hour health and fitness network, Jake is CEO of Body by Jake Enterprises, which develops products, programming, partnerships, and other multimedia endeavors promoting the benefits of a healthy lifestyle and a balanced and fulfilling life. He lives near Los Angeles with his wife and two children.

About the Type

This book was set in Sabon, a typeface designed by the well-known German typographer Jan Tschichold (1902–74). Sabon's design is based upon the original letter forms of Claude Garamond and was created specifically to be used for three sources: foundry type for hand composition, Linotype, and Monotype. Tschichold named his typeface for the famous Frankfurt typefounder Jacques Sabon, who died in 1580.